Men-at-Arms • 431

Britain's Secret War

The Indonesian Confrontation 1962–66

Will Fowler • Illustrated by Kevin Lyles
Series editor Martin Windrow

First published in Great Britain in 2006 by Osprey Publishing,
Midland House, West Way, Botley, Oxford OX2 0PH, UK
44-02 23rd St, Suite 219, Long Island City, NY 11101, USA
Email: info@ospreypublishing.com

© 2006 Osprey Publishing Ltd.

All rights reserved. Apart from any fair dealing for the purpose of
private study, research, criticism or review, as permitted under the
Copyright, Designs and Patents Act, 1988, no part of this publication
may be reproduced, stored in a retrieval system, or transmitted
in any form or by any means, electronic, electrical, chemical,
mechanical, optical, photocopying, recording or otherwise, without
the prior written permission of the copyright owner. Enquiries should
be addressed to the Publishers.

Transferred to digital print on demand 2010

First published 2006
3rd impression 2009

Printed and bound by PrintOnDemand-Worldwide.com,
Peterborough, UK

A CIP catalogue record for this book is available from the
British Library

ISBN: 978 1 84603 048 2

Editor: Martin Windrow
Page layouts by Alan Hamp
Typeset in New Baskerville and Helvetica
Maps by John Richards
Index by Glyn Sutcliffe
Originated by PPS Grasmere, Leeds, UK

The Woodland Trust
Osprey Publishing is supporting the Woodland Trust, the UK's
leading woodland conservation charity, by funding the
dedication of trees.

www.ospreypublishing.com

Artist's note
Readers may care to note that the original paintings from which the
colour plates in this book were prepared are available for private sale.
All reproduction copyright whatsoever is retained by the Publisher.
Enquiries should be addressed to:

Kevin Lyles
10 Cow Roast
Tring
Herts
HP23 5RF
UK

The Publishers regret that they can enter into no correspondence upon
this matter.

Select bibliography
Blaxland, Gregory, *The Regiments Depart,* William Kimber (London, 1971)
Cross, LtCol J.P., *'A Face like a Chicken's Backside',* Greenhill Books (London, 1996)
Cross, LtCol J.P., *Jungle Warfare,* Arms & Armour Press (London, 1989)
Dennis, Peter, & Jefrey Grey, *Emergency and Confrontation: Australian Military Operations in
    Malaya and Borneo 1950–66,* Allen & Unwin (NSW, Australia, 1996)
Dewar, Michael, *Brush Fire Wars,* Robert Hale (London, 1984)
Dickens, Peter, *SAS – The Jungle Frontier,* Arms & Armour Press (London, 1983)
Flintham, Victor, *Air Wars and Aircraft,* Arms & Armour Press (London, 1989)
Horner, David, *SAS – Phantoms of the Jungle,* Greenhill Books (London, 1991)
Jackson, Gen Sir William, *Withdrawal from Empire,* B.T.Batsford (London, 1986)
James, Harold, & Denis Sheil-Smith, *The Undeclared War,* Leo Cooper (London, 1971)
Ladd, James, *SBS – The Invisible Raiders,* Arms & Armour Press (London, 1983)
Ladd, James, *The Royal Marines,* Jane's (London, 1980)
McAlister, Gen R.W., *Bugle & Kukri,* Vol 2 (Regimental Trust,10th Princess Mary's Own
    Gurkha Rifles (1984)
Nasution, Gen Abdul Haris, *Fundamentals of Guerrilla Warfare,* Pall Mall Press (London, 1965)

BRITAIN'S SECRET WAR: THE INDONESIAN CONFRONTATION 1962-66

OPPOSITE **Two of the essential factors in the British victory in the Confrontation: Gurkha infantry, and a Fleet Air Arm Wessex helicopter, which has just dropped them on the helipad built outside a hilltop fort in Borneo. The foreground soldier carries an LMG field-modified with a forward pistol grip. (Royal Navy)**

THE POLITICAL BACKGROUND

THE WHOLE OF SOUTH-EAST ASIA saw dramatic changes between the mid 1950s and the early 1960s. Several former Dutch, French and British colonies in the region had become independent nations, some of them after bloody guerrilla campaigns, and were now asserting their newfound national identity. United States agencies had been involved in South Vietnam – formerly part of French Indochina – since 1954, and since 1961 US Army advisors had been assisting its government. By the end of 1964 there would be 23,000 US personnel in Vietnam, and the following March the first major ground units would arrive, beginning a commitment which would last seven grim years.

The former British colony of Malaya had been granted independence within the Commonwealth in August 1957, after the suppression of a nine-year communist guerrilla campaign (the 'Emergency') almost entirely limited to the large Chinese minority population. This had involved some 100,000 British and Gurkha troops with Australian, New Zealand and Malay support; but the new government was both stable and well inclined towards the West.[1]

Indonesia had achieved independence from the Netherlands in December 1949, but these hundreds of islands – stretching some 3,000 miles from west to east – were only partially controlled by the Djakarta government; their population of some 85 million, divided into 17 major ethnic groups, was riven by unrest. Nevertheless, in 1962 the president, Achmad Sukarno, an aggressive nationalist with pretensions to wider leadership among the 'non-aligned' nations, had a grandiose dream of forging a new Pacific union called 'Maphilindo', to bring together *Ma*laya, the *Phil*ippines and *Indo*nesia as a regional power bloc. This dream had been born in March 1945 when Sukarno had been a member of a body set up by the Japanese military administration of the occupied Netherlands East Indies.

The greater, southern part of the huge jungle island of Borneo (to the Indonesians, Kalimantan) lay within Indonesia; and initially Sukarno wished to extend his control over the neighbouring British colonies and protectorates in north-western Borneo – Sarawak, Sabah and the Sultanate of Brunei, known collectively as the North Borneo Territories – which were also approaching negotiated independence.

In May 1961 the Prime Minister of Malaya, Tunku Abdul Rahman, proposed that Malaya, the island state of Singapore and the North Borneo Territories should form a federation named Malaysia. Although at first sceptical, the British government saw the advantages that this plan offered, and the scheme would be acceptable to the United Nations. The

---
1 See Men-at-Arms 132, *The Malayan Campaign 1948–60*

Tunku was well qualified to lead Malaysia; an aristocratic British-educated lawyer, he had established his credentials both with Malayans as an anti-colonialist, and with the British as a staunch anti-communist. In Indonesia, Sukarno saw this move as a rebuff to his plans for Maphilindo. A flamboyant orator and 'headline addict', he started including in his public rants a slogan that would become his catchphrase: *'Ganjang Malaysia'* – 'Smash Malaysia'.

After many discussions the Federation of Malaysia was finally proclaimed on 16 September 1963 (though without the Sultanate of Brunei, which preferred sovereign independence). The Indonesian Foreign Minister, Dr Subandrio, then began making public references to a policy of Confrontation or *Konfrontasi* towards Malaysia, accusing the new state of being 'accomplices of neo-colonialist and neo-imperialist forces pursuing a policy hostile towards Indonesia'. In the words of Gen Sir William Jackson, 'He did not spell out what was meant by "confrontation", but it was assumed to be a blending of political, economic and military pressures just short of war.'

The Brunei revolt, December 1962

The first shots of the Confrontation pre-dated the formation of Malaysia. On 8 December 1962 a rebellion by members of the Kedayan tribe broke out in the oil-rich Sultanate of Brunei. The rebels adopted the title North Kalimantan National Army (*Tentara Nasional Kalimantan Utara* – TNKU); they were led by Yassin Affendi. The TNKU had about 4,000 followers in Brunei and Sarawak, but only some 150 of them were well armed and about 2,000 had shotguns. The rebellion would be suppressed quickly by men from four battalion-sized British infantry units: 1st Battalion, 2nd Gurkha Rifles (1/2nd GR), 42 Commando Royal Marines (42 Cdo RM), 1st Green Jackets (1 GJ), and the Queen's Own Highlanders (QOH).

At Brunei town, and at Limbang across the border in Sarawak, the TNKU had taken hostages, and there were indications that these would be executed on 12 December. In Singapore, 42 Cdo RM was warned to be ready to deploy to Brunei. Aircraft carried Gurkhas to Brunei town and Labuan island, which were quickly secured. On 10 December a Blackburn Beverley piloted by F/Lt Fenn carrying 90 men of the Queen's Own Highlanders landed at the rebel-held airstrip of Anduki in a *coup de main* operation. The control tower and police station were secured, two rebels killed and five captured. At Seria the QOH released 46 hostages, while Hawker Hunter jets of No.20 Sqn RAF kept the rebels' heads down with dummy strafing runs.

At Bakenu, over the border in Sarawak, 1 GJ suffered no casualties, killed five rebels and wounded six, and rounded up a further 328, from whom they recovered 327 shotguns. They were assisted by groups of local irregulars, subsequently led by Mr Tom Harrisson; now the curator of the Sarawak Museum, he had been parachuted into the Borneo jungle during World War II to organize resistance against the Japanese, and he knew and was trusted by the tribes.

Also on 10 December, L Coy, 42 Cdo RM commanded by Capt Jeremy Moore, MC, flew to Brunei town and prepared to move up-river to Limbang. Scant intelligence on the enemy suggested that they were about 150 strong, armed with shotguns, rifles and one Bren light machine gun. Against them Moore could commit two and a half troops of Marines (about 75 men), the Company HQ, and a section of .303in Vickers machine guns. In Brunei town the Marines found two old Z-lighters, ramp-loading barges that could be used as improvised landing craft. Before dawn on 12 December, flying the White Ensign and under Royal Navy crews from the coastal minesweepers HMS *Shawton* and *Fiskerton*, the lighters set sail for Limbang carrying the Marines. At that town, when about 300 yards from shore, they came under fire, which the Vickers crews returned. When the MGs on the second lighter were masked by the craft upstream, QMS Cyril Quoins asked Lt Peter Down RN if he would pull out of line astern to give him a clearer field of fire. 'Sergeant-major', came the reply, 'Nelson would have loved you!' – and the lighter moved into a more exposed position.

The first lighter beached 30 yards from the police station and the commandos stormed ashore. By chance the coxswain of the second lighter had been wounded, and the craft drifted past the landing point to beach 150 yards further

Bakenu, Sarawak, North Borneo Territories, December 1962: Rifleman Terry Fraser of 1st Green Jackets with a Union Flag shredded by the TNKU rebels. He wears the GJ rifle-green beret and silver crowned, wreathed Maltese Cross badge, OG shirt, OG trousers bloused over jungle boots, and the recently issued 58 Ptn web equipment; his 7.62mm L1A1 SLR is slung over his shoulder. (Imperial War Museum FES/62/263/54)

Brunei airport, December 1962: men of 1st Bn, Queen's Own Highlanders unloading stores from an RAF Blackburn Beverley C1 transport. During the Confrontation No 34 Sqn would operate Beverleys from Seletar and Labuan.

upstream near the hospital – where the hostages were being held. For the loss of five killed and six wounded (including a sailor) the hostages were rescued and the town secured. The rebels lost 15 killed and 50 captured; they had numbered 350, armed with automatic weapons, rifles and shotguns.

The Brunei revolt was effectively over by 17 December, but since it was sponsored by Indonesia it is now regarded as marking the beginning of the Confrontation. Lieutenant-Colonel H.J.Sweeney, MC, commanding 1 GJ, did not dismiss the TNKU rebels as a force: '[they] were extraordinarily well organized so far as knowing what to do, which vital installations to seize and the type of organization required to carry out a *coup d'etat*. They were organized in platoons, companies and battalions, they had a uniform of sorts, and their plans had been well laid. The rebellion failed initially to achieve its objects because of lack of weapons, the inept manner in which it was executed in spite of good plans, the unexpected resistance of the police… and poor leadership especially on the higher levels. To all this was added another important factor: the authorities at the last moment became suspicious and the police were standing-to.'

At the close of operations the units of 3 Cdo Bde received a signal from Capt S.R.Pringle RM, the Assistant Brigade Signals Officer, and Lt E.J.Oatley RM. This announced the institution of a medal for the campaign, and inattentive recipients must have reached Para Three before their suspicions were fully aroused as to the signal's status:

THREE. THE FACE SIDE OF THE BORNEO MEDAL BEARS AN ENGRAVING OF THE PROFILE OF THE KING OF DENMARK, AND THE REVERSE SIDE, AN ENGRAVED MESSAGE FROM GRATEFUL PEOPLE OF COPENHAGEN, DENMARKS CAPITAL CITY AND SITE OF THE EXPORT BOTTLING FACTORY OF CARLSBERG LAGER. THE RIBBON WILL BE BLOODSHOT RED WITH PINK ELEPHANTS AND LITTLE GREEN RATS SKILFULLY ENGRAVED UPON IT. THE MEDALS WILL BE ISSUED BY KELLOGS LTD. WHO WILL ENCLOSE THEM WITH A BALLOON AND SHERIFF'S STAR IN THEIR CORNFLAKE PACKETS.

CONFRONTATION

General Sir William Jackson described the three-and-a-half year conflict as a six-round contest, of which the Tunku and his British supporters won the first five rounds conclusively on points. He identified Round One as Sukarno's attempt to stop the creation of Malaysia; Round Two was the breaking of trade and diplomatic links, and the first cross-border raids by TNKU 'volunteers'; Round Three brought Indonesian political pressure through the United Nations, a peace conference in Bangkok in February 1964 during a short cease-fire, and the simultaneous deployment of regular Indonesian forces; Round Four saw operations by Indonesian regulars in Borneo and on the Malayan mainland, British cross-border raids in response, and peace talks in June 1964 in Tokyo. During Round Five in early 1965 Malaysia's position seemed momentarily to be shaken when Singapore withdrew from the Federation; but in Round Six, as Indonesia's economy spun out of control in the second half of 1965, internal dissension in Indonesia destroyed Sukarno and halted the Confrontation.

The main areas of operations would be the 900-mile border between Kalimantan (Indonesian Borneo), Sarawak, Brunei and Sabah. For operational control, Sarawak was divided by the British into five 'divisions', from the First Division in the west based on the capital of Kuching, to the Fifth Division on the Sabah border (note that these were simply operational areas, not 'divisions' in the sense of military formations). Sabah itself was divided into West, Central and East Brigade areas.

The British soldiers who fought in Malaysia were of a new generation – the post-National Service all-volunteer career army. Though the troops were the children of the post-war 'Baby Boom', their commanding officers had fought through World War II and Korea, and many company commanders and senior NCOs had gained jungle experience during the Malayan Emergency of the 1950s. When these officers and men deployed to the Far East they came as formed battalions, regiments or squadrons (not, like the US Army in Vietnam, as a trickle of conscripted individual reinforcements – a system which proved bad for morale and unit cohesion). The married men were accompanied by their families and accommodated in British-built married quarters, with Army schools for their children. The barracks, airfields and harbours built between the 1930s and 1950s were still available in Malaya, Singapore and Hong Kong as part of Britain's 'East of Suez' defence commitments. However, little of this infrastructure existed in Sabah and Sarawak, where roads, airstrips and accommodation would have to be improvised, improved or built from scratch.

General Walker's operational principles

The British and later Federation and Commonwealth forces who deployed to Borneo from 1963 were well served by the Director of Operations, MajGen Walter Walker, GOC 17th Gurkha Division and a veteran of the jungles of Burma and Malaya, who arrived in theatre in December 1962.

Walker's initial responsibility was to quash the Brunei rebellion; but he judged that there was a greater threat from Indonesia, and requested that at the close of that operation force levels in the

Seria, Brunei, 24 December 1962: MajGen Walter Walker, CBE, DSO (centre), GOC 17th Gurkha Inf Div and the newly appointed Director of Operations in the Borneo territories – to the soldiers patrolling the border he was 'Jungle Jim'. General Sir William Jackson described Walker as 'a strong, rather austere personality, who would only accept the highest professional standards and did not suffer fools gladly. He held crystal clear views on the policies to be pursued in North Borneo, about which he left no one in any doubt'. On the right is LtCol W.G.McHardy, MC, commanding 1st Queen's Own Highlanders, a veteran of North Africa who had also been badly wounded in Normandy. At left is Maj I.D.Cameron, commanding A Company. (IWM FES 62/264/28)

NORTH BORNEO BORDER AREA 1962–66

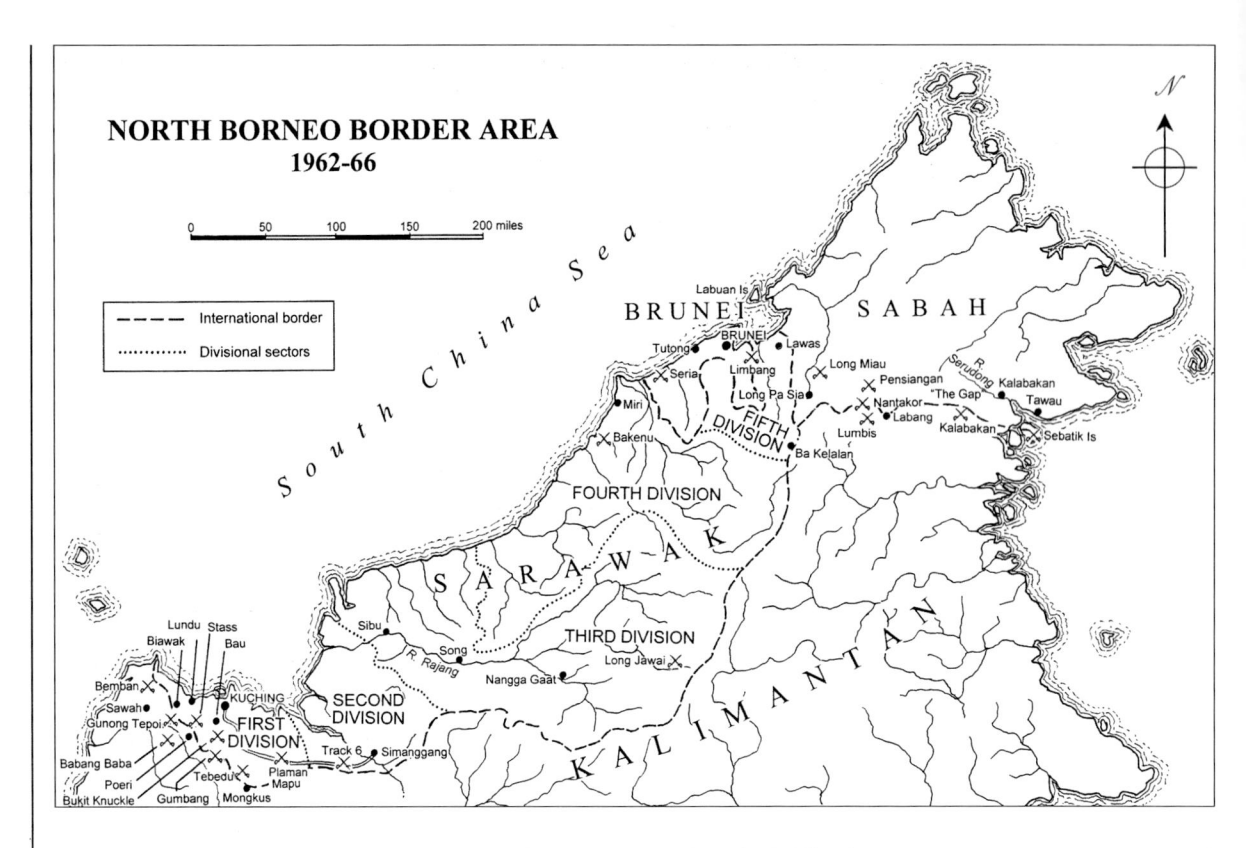

Throughout Borneo the inland terrain was characterized by steep ridges rising to 8,000ft mountains; thick rain forest, cast into perpetual gloom by the 100ft high jungle canopy; fast-flowing streams, and coastal mangrove swamps. There were very few motorable roads, and the climate ranged from stifling humidity to chill nights on which soldiers needed sleeping bags. Daily downpours of tropical rain added to the miseries of troops in the field, and restricted both movement on the ground and flights by helicopters.

area should not be reduced. Walker's assessment was correct, and operations would soon have to be undertaken first to contain cross-border raids by IBTs – 'Indonesia-based Border Terrorists' – and later to destroy their will to launch them. In his first operations directive Walker laid down the six principles which would guide the prosecution of the campaign:

(1) Joint operations between the police and the three armed services
(2) Timely and accurate intelligence information
(3) Speed, mobility and flexibility
(4) Security of bases
(5) Domination of the jungle
(6) Winning and keeping the confidence of the indigenous people.

The Police Special Branch, working with the Army, was able to supply information about local terrorist leaders and their likely hiding places in Sarawak and Sabah. Thanks to this intelligence, Yassin Affendi, the last of the surviving TNKU leaders, who had set up a base in swamps on the bank of the Brunei river near Kampong Serdang, was eliminated. Men of the 2/7th Gurkha Rifles swept through his camp at dawn on 18 May 1963, and Yassin Affendi was fatally wounded when his party ran into a cut-off group positioned outside the camp.

'Hearts and minds' – 22 SAS

Among the units under his command Gen Walker had A Sqn, 22nd Special Air Service Regiment. His original plan for their employment was as a mobile 'fire brigade' which could parachute into the jungle to recapture any border villages seized by the Indonesians. The commanding officer of 22 SAS, LtCol John Woodehouse, felt that this would result in heavy casualties and was a poor use of skilled men. Woodehouse had joined the British Army as a private in 1941; he, Michael Calvert and Dare Newell were the three men who had transformed the Malayan Scouts into 22 SAS in the early 1950s. Woodehouse, with a fund of practical experience to draw upon, proposed to Walker that the SAS should operate in small patrols along the jungle border as 'eyes and ears', while gaining the confidence of the local tribal groups – thus achieving both items (2) and (6) on Walker's list of principles.

The SAS patrols were deployed about every 60 miles along the border, and immediately began a 'hearts and minds' programme among the tribal villages of the Dyaks, Muruts, Kelabits and Punans. For the local population there were real benefits from the relationship, since the antibiotics carried by the SAS medics could sometimes cure overnight simple medical conditions from which the patients had endured months of distress. Apart from routine medical assistance, the resourceful SAS teams made themselves popular in many other ways (one enterprising sergeant named 'Gypsy' Smith built a miniature hydro-electric plant in a stream at Talibakus, Sabah, and provided the only electric lighting for 370 miles). Between January and April 1963, A Sqn operated with only 70 men in theatre, but by breaking their four-man patrols down to two or three men they were able to send out 21 patrols. They remained out in the jungle for up to six months, living with small tribal communities. By the time the Indonesians began large scale incursions in April 1963 the tripwire was in place and reporting enemy movements.

With his forces stretched to the limit, Gen Walker authorized the arming and training of tribesmen from communities close to the Kalimantan border as a 'home guard' force called the Border Scouts. Under the leadership and guidance of men of the SAS and Gurkha Independent Parachute Company, the Scouts became 'one thousand pairs of eyes and ears' providing useful intelligence, since they were able to move freely across the borders. One of the men selected to advise on formation of the Border Scouts was Tom Harrisson, the World War II veteran whose detailed local knowledge had already proved valuable in the Brunei revolt.

'Hearts and minds' operations were conducted by all front line units; recalling the distribution of medical aid to the Dyaks in 1964, 2/Lt Robert Pasley-Tyler of 3 GJ wrote: 'I think that it would be fair to say that only about … 40 per cent of the sick treated were genuine. The other 60 per cent just liked our pills.' Lieutenant N.E.Shaw of 1 GJ, writing in 1962 about contacts with the Kelabits, reflected an affection and respect for them which was widespread among the soldiers: 'What marks life in a Kelabit longhouse is its freedom and lack of rules. They are an easy-living people; children can do anything they want to, a girl can marry whom she wants. Even the dogs, within reason, have the freedom of the longhouse… The easy-going friendship was extended to us soldiers. We

'Hearts and minds' in a tribal village, 1965: a medical orderly from the Queen's Dragoon Guards cleans a woman's cut hand before dressing it. The phrase 'hearts and minds' had first been used by FM Sir Gerald Templer in his campaign against Communist Terrorists (CTs) in Malaya, 1952–56, when troops under his command had won the loyal assistance of jungle tribes as intelligence-gatherers and guides. The concept would prove even more effective in Borneo, where it was initiated by 22 SAS but pursued by all front-line units. The soldiers' medical kits could make a huge difference in remote villages which had never had access to modern treatment, but it was so popular that everyone wanted pills whether they were sick or not. The Royal Ulster Rifles discovered that a Smarties chocolate bean rapidly cured many a notionally 'sick' child and sent them away happy. (IWM FEW/65/59/3)

**1964: LtCol Kellway-Bamber, CO of 1st Argyll & Sutherland Highlanders, inspects Border Scouts attached to his A Company. These Ibans are fully uniformed and equipped, and armed with SLRs; the man at far left has a tribal tattoo emerging from under his shirtsleeve, and the word 'Iban' on his forearm. The initial Border Scout programme was frustrated by political and financial difficulties, and the recruitment of the wrong men (by no means all tribesmen were born warriors); but they were steadily improved by the energetic commitment of Maj John Cross, an experienced 7th Gurkhas officer. Hand-picked by Gen Walker, this veteran jungle soldier produced impressive results by early 1965.
Other Scottish units deployed during the Confrontation and not already mentioned in the body text were 1st Gordon Highlanders and 1st King's Own Scottish Borderers. (IWM FEB 64/42/39)**

were not held in awe because we were white and strange. We were men who could talk, become friends, take and give presents, we were people who could amuse them too.'

In February 1965, 1 Sqn, Australian SAS Regt (SASR) deployed to Brunei, and in March sent out the first operational patrols on Operation 'Keen Edge' (see 'Australian SAS', below). This operation combined jungle familiarization with a hearts-and-minds programme; and a report by 2/Lt Trevor Roderick describes two of the Border Scouts. While Sgt John Iban Ngerong was 'very intelligent, strong and healthy', another Scout was a 'lazy con man but quite a character. Useful for small jobs and interpreter, speaks limited English and Malay. Bachelor and lecherous bloke, likes his sex and grog and worships Dollars. A swift kick now and then might help him. I keep scaring Christ out of him, when I tell him I am going to take him over the border'. Like a good Australian, Roderick made a cricket bat and his patrol instructed the villagers in the rudiments of the game. However, the real assistance was medical, and his patrol medic Pte Bruce English treated cuts and minor injuries, flu and chickenpox, and even assisted at a childbirth. Other medics found that penicillin worked very effectively, while WO Thompson reported that 'a distribution of vitamin pills, ointment and Elastoplast goes over well... They have supplied us with a couple of meals of curried squirrel (very good), curried chicken and rice'.

Summary of Commonwealth forces

In December 1962, Gen Walker had just one brigade of three infantry battalions, and six *Ton* Class coastal minesweepers. These little 360-ton warships – with a crew of 29, one 40mm Bofors and two 20mm Oerlikon guns – were invaluable for patrolling the 1,500 miles of Borneo's coastline and estuaries. Walker also had 15 Fleet Air Arm (FAA) and RAF helicopters, which were to play a critical part in the campaign. After Malaysian statehood in September 1963, Walker's forces were augmented by the 3rd & 5th Bns, Royal Malay Regiment (RMR), and the Federal Reconnaissance Regiment.

When Walker handed over command in March 1965 to MajGen George Lea, his multi-national force consisted of 17,000 men of whom over half were British and the remainder Gurkha, Malay, Australian or New Zealanders; and out on the jungle border there were another 1,500 tribal Border Scouts. At any one time British Far East Land Forces had about 18 battalions of British and Gurkha infantry, either under Walker's direct command or available at need. He had two regiments of Saladin armoured cars armed with 76mm guns, engineers, and artillery with 5.5in (140 mm) medium guns and 105mm pack howitzers. The British and Commonwealth air forces had at any one time about 80 helicopters and 40 fixed wing aircraft, including Hawker Hunter and Gloster Javelin jet fighters. Off-shore were a Royal Navy force of aircraft or helicopter carriers, destroyers, frigates, coastal minesweepers, fast patrol boats – and at Tawau, Sabah, even Saunders Roe SRN5 hovercraft.

The Malayan, North Borneo and Sarawak Police Field Forces and Special Branch played a major part in gathering intelligence; here an officer inspects a unit of about 20 Border Scouts. These men are armed with the .303in rifle No.5 Mk 1 or 'jungle carbine', which was issued to the Scouts in some numbers. This cut-down weapon was unpopular with British troops for its vicious kick, muzzle blast, and unreliable sights. At far left, an NCO wears the 'Border Scouts' shoulder title (see Plate H2), and the hornbill shoulder patch devised by Maj John Cross. (RM Museum)

This IBT being escorted to the terminal building at Sibu airport in Third Division seems to have multiple light wounds. The soldier guarding him is carrying the prisoner's Sten SMG and web pouches. General Walker had leaflets dropped over the border area and approach routes, offering safe conduct to Indonesians and local guerrillas who chose to surrender 'before you are killed by the Security Forces, or before you die of disease or starvation in the jungle'. (IWM HU 72775)

INDONESIAN CROSS-BORDER ATTACKS, 1963–64

The first clash came on 12 April 1963, when IBTs attacked a police station at Tebedu in south-west Sarawak; although the raiders were repulsed by Insp Chimbon's men, the IBTs looted the local bazaar. Eleven days later 15 IBTs attacked a police post at Gumbang in Sarawak's First Division, held by a half-section from C Coy, 40 Cdo Royal Marines. They returned fire, killing two IBTs and wounding three; one Marine was slightly wounded. These small-scale raids set the style for operations which were intended to intimidate the police and destroy their influence on the border.

The Special Branch discovered that a group called the Clandestine Communist Organization (CCO) was established in western Sarawak. Captured suspects talked of weapons training, as well as plans for attacks on police stations and ambushes against the security forces. The CCO would provide the Indonesians with an indigenous 'front' for their raids; and Djakarta named their raiders the TNKU – North Kalimantan National Army – ostensibly the heirs of the original Brunei rebels. Although the first raids did include CCO members, they were led by regular Indonesian officers or NCOs from the Marine commandos – *Korps Komando Operasi* (KKO); the Army para-commandos – *Regimen Para Kommando Angaton Darat* (RPKAD); and the Air Force paratroops – *Pasukan Gerak Tjepat* (PGT).

Long Jawai, September–October 1963

On 28 September 1963 about 150 IBTs crossed into the Third Division and attacked a small outpost at Long Jawai garrisoned by six soldiers from 1/2nd Gurkha Rifles, three policemen and 21 Border Scouts. Under fire from automatic weapons and a 60mm mortar the garrison suffered casualties and were forced to withdraw; seven Border Scouts were captured and later murdered. The Indonesians had scored a small victory, but were now 50 miles inside Sarawak. The CO of 1st/2nd GR, the

Imphal veteran LtCol Clements, MC, used FAA Wessex helicopters from 845 Naval Air Squadron (NAS) to position ambushes on likely exit routes.

On 1 October the Gurkhas got their first payback: an ambush commanded by Lt Pasbahadur caught two Indonesian longboats and sank one, killing 26 IBTs; from the other the radio sets from Long Jawai were recovered, along with the 60mm mortar. Survivors from the longboats were killed in an ambush on 10 October, and a staging camp was located two days later. Three Indonesians were also killed as they attempted to shoot down a helicopter operating close to the border. The Gurkhas' tactics were to set the style for containment operations: ambushes were set to catch IBTs either on their way in for an attack, if intelligence allowed this; or on their way out as they ran for the border. A veteran of these operations explained that with a few exceptions this inevitably meant that IBT raids were of short duration, and so did not penetrate deep into Malaysian territory.

Kalabakan, December 1963–January 1964

The Indonesians had concentrated their efforts on Sarawak, but in mid December 1963 they decided to launch a large scale attack against Tawau, the capital of Sabah, and the town of Kalabakan. General Walker had anticipated that raids might be launched across the coastal border of Sabah, and men of Nos.2 & 6 Sections of the RM Special Boat Squadron (SBS) – working with 40 Cdo RM – patrolled the Serudong river and Sebatik island on the east coast. In 1963 they had set up the Tawau Assault Group (TAG), a riverine force based at the mouth of the Serudong and operating from civilian cabin cruisers, dories and native longboats as well as SBS Klepper canoes.

The Indonesian force assembled for the attack consisted of 128 men, mostly volunteers, with 35 Indonesian KKO marines and NCOs. They were divided into four detachments: N1 – KKO Sgt Benny, with eight KKO and 28 guerrillas; N2 – Wayang, with 15 KKO and 21 guerrillas; W1 – Lasani, with 34 men; and W2, KKO Sgt Buronto with 22 men. They crossed the border on 21 December, and a week later were close to Kalabakan. N1 attacked a 3rd RMR post, whose defences had not been completed; the IBTs were able to crawl within grenade range, killing eight soldiers including the company commander and wounding 19 troops. Another attack on the police station caused no casualties, but N1 and N2 lingered in the area – which was to prove a fatal mistake.

Lieutenant-Colonel Burnett brought in B & C Coys of his 1/10th Gurkha Rifles, and while Kalabakan was dug and wired for defence, smaller communities were evacuated and commercial transport centralized, to deny food and mobility to the IBTs. By 5 January 1964 ambushes were in position covering the likely withdrawal routes; and between 7 and 17 January the Gurkhas killed 15 IBTs and captured six from N1 and N2. By February, four IBTs from W1 were dead and the remaining 12 scattered in two groups.

An IBT (right) is brought into a helicopter LZ, probably at Nangga Gaat in Sarawak's Third Division, by three less formally dressed Border Scouts, armed with single-barrel 12 bore shotguns.
The Cross-Border Scouts, a force of 40 specially selected Iban tribesmen, was raised by the SAS in summer 1964. They were trained by Maj John Edwards of A Sqn, who led them until the end of hostilities. From August 1964 they were active in western Sarawak; and it was their reports of numerous Indonesian soldiers in villages around Bemban across the border in Kalimantan that identified these *kampongs* as staging posts for cross-border raids into First Division. (Royal Navy)

W2, attempting to escape through the mangrove swamps, encountered the TAG, which was supported at night by RAF aircraft and RN ships dropping flares and firing starshell. By the end of February, 96 of the 128 IBTs had been killed or captured; 20 had managed to regain Indonesian territory, and the 12 still at large had little hope of survival. Significantly, at least 21 of the 35 KKO marines had been accounted for, and the NCOs Lasani and Wayang had been killed. The Kalabakan attack prompted the British government to make more troops available for operations.

Posed photo found on the body of an IBT. The centre man seems to be making a political point; those on either side aim Lee Enfield rifles – an SMLE and a No.4. They seem to wear a motley mixture of British or Dutch and US uniform and webbing. The Clandestine Communist Organization and other individuals who had volunteered, been press-ganged on the border, or even released from Indonesian jails, were formed into units called *Pramukas*, but these were often ill trained and poorly motivated. The Indonesians would eventually accept that the Confrontation could only be pursued effectively by their regular troops. (RM Museum)

Long Miau and the Rajang river, January 1964

Close to Sabah in the Sarawak Fifth Division, on 23 January 1964, a ten-man patrol of the 1st Royal Leicesters under Lt Michael Peele attacked 40 Indonesians as they lunched in a clearing north of Long Miau. The patrol had been directed into the area after Sgt Bob Creighton of D Sqn, 22 SAS had picked up the tracks of military boots (D Sqn had relieved A Sqn in May 1963). Peele's attack killed five enemy and forced the rest to flee, abandoning half a ton of arms and ammunition. When Sgt Creighton searched the site he found two survivors, who confirmed that the group had been intending to cross into Brunei.

In a small scale but tough operation in early January men of the 1/7th Gurkhas and the Special Branch co-operated in eliminating a group of 23 IBTs commanded by an Indonesian sergeant, who had landed by boat in the mangrove swamps of an estuary in eastern Sabah. Realizing that their landing had been compromised, they split up; one group of seven was destroyed by Gurkhas led by Maj D.O'Leary, operating from a requisitioned launch with the apt name *The Jolly Bachelor*. For three Gurkhas wounded, they killed three raiders, wounded two and captured one, with an LMG, a Sten and two Armalites. The remainder of the Indonesian group were later captured hiding on a stolen fishing boat.

*   *   *

Talks in Bangkok, Thailand, between Malaysia and Indonesia under United Nations chairmanship produced a truce which lasted from 25 January to 6 March 1964. Foreign Minister Subandrio insisted that the cross-border raids were the work of local volunteers, beyond the control of Djakarta. Tun Razak, representing Malaysia, insisted that all infiltrators should be withdrawn before substantive negotiations could start. The talks dragged on, but by the first week of March three groups of between 30 and 50 IBTs had crossed the borders: into the First

Division at Lundu at the end of January, at Bau on 21 February and at Rassau on 6 March. On each occasion they were intercepted by 42 Cdo RM or 1/2nd GR, and suffered casualties before they withdrew.

Track 6, March 1964
With the breakdown of the Bangkok talks the Indonesians attempted to push back the recognized border by occupying and holding commanding hill features just inside Sarawak. On 7 March a fierce action took place on Track 6 on the edge of the Kling-Kang range in the Second Division; two Gurkhas of the 2/10th were killed as they approached an Indonesian position. The Indonesians withdrew, leaving one dead (though more were certainly carried off) and much booty; documents indicated that the camp had held 40 men from the regular 328 Para-Raider Battalion. Radio intercepts picked up 328 Bn reports that they had a lot of dead and wounded and were in considerable difficulties. The reply from their headquarters was brief and brutal: basically, 'Get on with it – there are plenty more where they came from'.

Some days later the Indonesians returned to the ridge some 16 miles to the eastward. This time Maj Mayman, commanding A Coy, 2/10th GR, was supported by two Wessex helicopters firing French wire-guided Nord SS11 missiles, a troop of 105mm pack howitzers from 70 Bty RA, and the 76mm guns of two Saladin armoured cars from Queen's Royal Irish Hussars. Even so the Gurkhas had a hard fight to dislodge the Indonesians, who left two dead when they withdrew.

* * *

There were no fewer than 34 similar attacks along the border during summer 1964. In Operation 'Sabre Tooth' the Gurkhas of 2/10th hunted down a platoon-strength Indonesian patrol of the so-called Black Cobra Battalion, commanded by Maj Audy Patawari, which had crossed the border at the end of March. The Cobras blundered into a Gurkha ambush which resulted in the loss of their packs containing food and ammunition. By April, Gurkha patrols had accounted for 27 out of the 36 raiders.[2]

On 20 May 1964, President Sukarno boasted that he would crush Malaysia 'by the time the sun rises on 1 January 1965'. Reports came

A Royal Marine patrol boards two requisitioned civilian cabin cruisers in Brunei town. In 1963 the Special Boat Service used such craft – alongside small native boats and their own two-man Klepper canoes – when they set up the Tawau Assault Group (TAG) at the mouth of the Serudong river on the east coast of Sabah. The further launch, flying the White Ensign, has an LMG set up on the bow surrounded by piled packs. More conventional Royal Navy warships deployed 'in Borneo waters' included at various dates 5 aircraft carriers, 2 commando (helicopter) carriers, 1 cruiser, 7 destroyers, 15 frigates and 19 coastal minesweepers – 7 of the latter manned by RNZN crews. (IWM FES 62/261/85)

---
2 For what it may be worth – the Royal Marines Museum at one time held a pentagonal metal badge, perhaps from a cap: a white rim, around a yellow field bearing a black cobra coiled to strike, above 'SARAWAK'.

A Saladin armoured car of 4th Royal Tank Regt, working closely with an Auster AOP 9 of 16 Flight, AAC, during a road patrol in a low-lying area of Sarawak in 1964. The Saladin bears the divisional sign of 17th British Div – a black cat on a yellow background.

The Royal Armoured Corps were noted for their versatility; apart from road patrols they worked with the infantry and SAS, patrolled rivers in canoes, and carried out 'hearts & minds' programmes in the villages. Besides 4 RTR, the Life Guards, Queen's Dragoon Guards, Queen's Royal Irish Hussars and 5 RTR all served in theatre at various dates during the campaign. (IWM FES 64/331/1)

in of a steady build-up of Indonesian Marine commandos and of paratroopers in camps in Kalimantan, on the Sumatra coast opposite the Malayan mainland, and on the Riau Islands south of Singapore. Faced by this threat, Gen Walker received 51 Bde of the Strategic Reserve, with its HQ and one Gurkha and two British battalions. Walker was now able to rotate and redeploy battalions, and he established three brigade sectors: 99 Gurkha Bde (having relieved 3 Cdo Bde) became West Brigade, with five battalions holding Kuching and the three western divisions of Sarawak; 51 Bde took over as Central Brigade, with two battalions holding the rest of Sarawak and Brunei; and 5 Malaysian Bde, based at Tawau, had three battalions holding Sabah as Eastern Brigade.

MAINLAND RAIDS, 1964–65

In June 1964 a bomb placed by an Indonesian infiltrator damaged an Avro Shackleton of 205 Sqn RAF at Changi, Singapore; this marked a change of tactics by the Indonesians. On 17 August the first of a series of raids by sea and air was launched against the Malayan Peninsula – 'West Malaysia'.

The first group consisted of 53 Air Force paratroops (PGT), 21 marines (KKO), 32 Malaysians (of whom 27 were Chinese communists) and two Indonesian volunteers. The plan was to land 45 men from the sea north of the Sanglang river near Benut, 33 at Pontian Kechil, and 30 to the south at Kukup. Once they were ashore they would establish a base at Gunong Pulai about 12 miles inland, to conduct guerrilla operations, and would later link up with paratroops who would be dropped near Labis in northern Johore. The hopes for this and subsequent Indonesian landings were predicated on active support by the local population. Remarkably, the Indonesians had convinced themselves that Malaysia was ripe for revolution and would welcome them as 'liberators'. There had in fact been several days of inter-racial rioting in Singapore in late July 1964, resulting in 22 deaths and many injuries – but this was emphatically not a pro-Indonesian insurrection.

The Pontian Kechil group came under fire from a police post as soon as they landed; they scattered, abandoning much of their equipment. The west coast of Malaya went on to the alert, and in under a week all but four of the group had been captured. The Benut group encountered Malaysian forces and suffered four casualties; the survivors went into hiding, but between 2 and 23 October the security forces killed their leader and tracked down all but a few. The Kukup group was discovered within 48 hours of landing, and eliminated apart from four marines, who escaped back to Sumatra in mid September. There was some low level sabotage in Malaya and Singapore.

On the night of 1/2 September 1964 four C-130B Hercules transports each carrying 48 men took off on Operation *'Dwikova'*. The force consisted of 151 PGT paratroops and 41 Malaysian Chinese communists. Bad weather and engine trouble forced two aircraft to turn back. The first group landed at 01.45 on the wrong drop zone and were unable to recover their weapons, rations and equipment containers, which were found by the police. The second group landed on the correct DZ in thick jungle, and roped down from the tree canopy, but could not find their containers. A state of emergency was declared in Malaya on 2 September, and air defences including Bristol Bloodhound SAMs of No 65 Sqn, RAF Javelin and RAAF Sabre fighters were deployed; the destroyer HMS *Kent* was stationed in the Straits of Malacca to cover the radar gap between Bukit Gombak and Butterworth through which the Indonesian C-130s had been able to penetrate.

The 1/10th Gurkhas and 1st Bn Royal New Zealand Regt (1 RNZR) were alerted to hunt the paratroops. RAF Hawker Hunters flew 14 sorties on the first day, rocketing suspect areas. For some of the Gurkhas based at Labis police station this was familiar territory; they had hunted CTs in the area during the Emergency. 'Many old hands of the Battalion were there, only a little bit older, wiser and more rotund, but their keenness still not blunted… Like terriers on a rat hunt, the Battalion converged on Labis and then scuttled off into the jungle on the scent'.

The Gurkhas and 1 RNZR patrolled for a month, and between 7 and 9 September the Gurkhas killed five paratroopers and captured two. On the 13th they suffered their first casualty when a lance-corporal was killed in a firefight in which four more Indonesians were killed and seven captured. At dawn on 23 September, Maj R.Haddow was killed in an encounter in which all the Indonesians were killed. Intelligence from the captured paratroops gave the hunters detailed information with which to work. It was believed that a charismatic Indonesian paratrooper, SgtMaj Wogimen, was still at large. By October 1964, however, when 1/10th GR were withdrawn from the hunt after accounting for 51 of the raiders, they 'were forced to the regretful conclusion that Wogimen was still hanging from his parachute in one of the trees somewhere in the jungle'.

On 29 October, 52 Indonesians landed at the mouth of the Kesang river on the Johore-Malacca state boundary, but were spotted by fishermen. A tight cordon was quickly put in place by the police, 3rd Bn Royal Australian Regt (3 RAR) and 1 RNZR; within 30 hours 50 raiders had surrendered, and the last two, exhausted and starving, were captured three weeks later.

Two more major landing attempts were made along the west coast. On 23 December, 28 Indonesians landed south-west of Johore; within a short time they were cornered in thick mangrove swamps, and Operation 'Birdsong' was launched. Sycamore helicopters of 103 Sqn RAF acted as forward air controllers for Hunters and Canberras. Three infiltrators were killed and the rest surrendered. On 24 December, 61 Indonesians attempted a landing north-west of Kuala Lumpur. An Indonesian armed customs launch lifted them to an island in the Malacca Straits, and then pirated ten Malaysian fishing boats from One Fathom Bank to carry the raiders on the final stage of their journey. The convoy was intercepted by

Every battalion serving in the jungle had trained patrol and tracker dogs, which could detect the presence of the enemy ahead, or could follow up blood trails. Infantry patrol dogs and trackers were worked either on a long lead, or loose; when loose they generally roamed about 30 yards ahead, seeking scents. Great care had to be taken that the dog did not become exhausted; Labradors proved the best trackers, capable of working by day and night for about two days at a time, and Alsatians (German Shepherds) were also used as patrol dogs. When they smelt or heard an approaching or concealed enemy they would 'point'. This dog is leading a patrol by 2nd Green Jackets. (IWM FEW 65/32/60)

the frigate HMS *Ajax*; the fishing boats were captured, with large stocks of ammunition and explosives, but the launch escaped.

The Indonesians also attempted landings on the coastline south-east of Johore. Between 7 November 1964 and 25 March 1965 they made five landings; the first two, in November and December, were quickly mopped up. On the night of 25/26 February, 44 Indonesian police and volunteers came ashore and ambushed men of the Singapore Regt, killing eight and wounding five. By the end of March, however, the security forces had accounted for all 44 infiltrators. Two more attempted landings were quickly foiled, as well as several minor incursions. On 31 March 1965 the total number of attempted landings stood at 41, with 142 Indonesians killed and 309 captured. On 30 May, in a final gesture, 25 Indonesian regular soldiers landed at Tanjong Pen-Gelih in eastern Johore and occupied a position built by the Japanese in World War II. A day later they surrendered, after strikes by rocket-firing Hunters.

Australian and New Zealand commitment, 1965–66

The landings on the Malay Peninsula had wider repercussions than Sukarno had anticipated. The Australian government had been reluctant to provide military assistance, because it shared a long border with Indonesia on the huge island of New Guinea; the western half was Indonesian 'West Irian', and the eastern half Austalian-protected Papua-New Guinea. They had troops based in Malaya as part of 28th Commonwealth Inf Bde of the Far East Strategic Reserve; but these were intended only to protect Malaya against external attack.

During the cordon-and-search operations following Indonesian raids on the mainland men of 3 RAR and 1 RNZR were employed, since these were clearly external attacks. The Australian and New Zealand governments now agreed that troops should be committed to Borneo, and in March 1965, 3 RAR arrived in Sarawak, where it served until the end of July. During this time the Australians mounted extensive operations on both sides of the border, and had four major contacts with the Indonesians. In May an ambush commanded by Lt Patrick Beale caught four Indonesian boats. Two were destroyed; the third was visible to only one soldier, Pte Jackson, but he engaged it with his rifle and killed all five occupants. Jackson hurled grenades at the fourth boat, and to get a better shot at it he climbed a tree. When Lt Beale ordered the withdrawal, the platoon had killed at least 15 Indonesians.

On 12 July 1965 an ambush commanded by 2/Lt Byers caught 25 Indonesians in the killing ground; when it was sprung 17 enemy were killed, but the survivors counter-attacked, and in the subsequent ten-minute firefight two Australians were wounded. Calling down artillery fire, Byers was then able to withdraw his platoon.

In 1966, 3 RAR were replaced by 4 RAR, whose tour in Sarawak between April and August was quieter, but who also operated on both sides of the border.

September 1964: the Indonesian landings on the Malayan mainland led to a heightened state of alert as the war threatened to escalate to an entirely new level. An RAF Whirlwind HAR 10 circles Ferret scout cars of C Sqn, Queen's Royal Irish Hussars. The regiment had three sabre squadrons each of three troops, each troop equipped with two Saladin six-wheel heavy armoured cars with 76mm guns and 2x .30in MGs, and two MG-armed Ferret Mk II scout cars; a separate 'assault troop' rode in Saracen armoured personnel carriers.
The RAF operated Whirlwinds of Nos 103, 110 & 230 Sqns in detachments based at various locations. Other Commonwealth helicopter assets were the UH-1B 'Hueys' of No 5 Sqn RAAF, and the Alouette IIIs of No 5 Sqn RMAF. (IWM R 29872)

In addition to 3 and 4 RAR, and two squadrons of the Australian SASR (see below), Australia deployed several artillery batteries and troops of Royal Australian Engineers. In all, 23 Australians were killed during the Confrontation and eight wounded.

THE CONFRONTATION IN THE AIR

The first helicopters to arrive in Borneo were Bristol Belvederes of No.66 Sq RAF, as well as various detachments of Westland Whirlwinds. The FAA contributed four squadrons flying the Westland Wessex and Whirlwind, and the Army Air Corps (AAC) five Scout and five Sioux flights. Though higher figures have been quoted, Gen Jackson states that there were never more than 70 helicopters available in theatre at any one time. Sheil-Small and James suggest that 'had six helicopters been available per battalion, Confrontation might well have finished a year earlier'. The jungle workhorses were unquestionably the Wessex and the Scout. The Wessex HAS Mk 1 could carry up to 16 troops, with a range of 645 miles; the Scout AH Mk 1 could carry four troops plus the pilot and co-pilot; it had a range of 312 miles.

Though all the RAF, AAC and FAA fixed- and rotary-wing crews were critical for the supplying of forward troops and inserting and extracting them from the jungle, the naval airmen of 845 NAS made a particularly significant contribution. Between December 1962, when they first went ashore, and early 1965 the squadron completed 10,000 hours' flying, carried over 50,000 passengers and 6,000,000lbs of stores, and evacuated 500 casualties – 40 of them at night in tropical rainstorms. Under LtCdr G.J.Sherman, half of this Wessex squadron went ashore split into three detachments. The headquarters was at Sibu (which like any RN shore establishment was given a ship's name – HMS *Hornbill*), and the other detachments were posted to Nangga Gaat and Simanggang in the Second and Third Divisions. The other half of the squadron remained aboard the commando carriers HMS *Bulwark* and HMS *Albion*, with each group rotating every three months.

During operations 845 NAS lost five aircraft with three pilots, two aircrewmen and 11 soldiers in accidents in February, March and April 1965. By then the squadron had such a close relationship with the Ibans of Nangga Gaat that the villagers voluntarily went into mourning for a month; during this period no gongs were beaten and, though cheerfully sociable, the Ibans held none of their usual parties.

The famous London *Evening Standard* cartoonist 'JAK' visited 845 NAS among various British units in Borneo during the Confrontation. One cartoon shows himself as a pale, bespectacled figure in a longboat crewed by a tattooed Iban, arriving at a landing stage on a jungle river to be greeted by a bunch of bearded toughs dressed in nothing but sarongs, with beads around their necks, spears in their hands and

Men from 1/10th Gurkha Rifles – note white recognition sign on hats – bring in one of the 96 Indonesian paratroopers dropped near Labis, Malaya, on the night of 1/2nd September 1964. He appears to wear plain olive drab; other prisoners wore the camouflage uniform shown in Plate A2. This Gurkha battalion accounted for 51 of the raiders. (Maj H.E.Shields)

RAF & Commonwealth air force combat squadrons deployed at various dates during the Confrontation

RAF
Nos 20 & 28 (Hunter GA9)
Nos 60 & 64 (Javelin F9)
No 45 (Canberra B15)
No 81 (Canberra PR7)
No 205 (Shackleton MR2)

RAAF
Nos 3 & 75 (F-86 Sabre)
No 2 (Canberra B)

RNZAF
No 14 (Canberra B)

parangs (native machetes) at their belts; one of these desperadoes has a small monkey clinging to his neck and a Royal Navy beret on his head.

In September 1963, Indonesian Air Force (AURI) B-25s escorted by P-51s from Potiak in Kalimantan made nine incursions over Sarawak. A year later B-25s and B-26s launched hit-and-run attacks against isolated *kampongs*. Although the much faster Gloster Javelin jets of Nos.60 & 64 Sqns attempted interceptions, they had only one success over Borneo, confronting a C-130 which escaped over the border. Over Singapore the Javelins intercepted a Tu-16 and escorted it out of the area. The Indonesians had more success with anti-aircraft artillery, which they established on the border and on the Riau Islands just south of Singapore. The first British aircraft to be lost to Indonesian AAA was an Auster AOP.9 on 28 December 1963 at Lundu; the wounded Sgt Thakeray managed to land on a helicopter LZ. In 1965 the air traffic controllers at Changi Airport, Singapore re-routed civilian and military aircraft to avoid the Riau Islands, and none was hit by AAA; however, on 17 November 1965 the Indonesians shot down a Whirlwind of No.103 Sqn near Stass in the First Division.

An RAF Bristol Belvedere HC 1 of No.66 Sqn is loaded with stores by men of 176 Bty Royal Artillery at a forward position in Sarawak; in the foreground, a 105mm pack howitzer is readied for lifting as an underslung load. Given the need for flexibility and speed of response, Gen Walker decentralized his artillery and air assets. Guns were deployed in ones and twos to the jungle forts in Borneo, and one gun per battery was held in reserve, ready to be lifted forward by helicopter at need. The Belvederes of No 66 were based at Kuching. (IWM FEW 65/24/12)

TACTICS

JUNGLE FORTS

Soon after the TNKU raid against Tebedu in April 1963, Brig F.C.Barton, commanding 3 Cdo Bde Group, initiated a fort construction programme along the border between Sarawak and Kalimantan, to cover all the likely 'gates' into and out of Malaysia. The programme was endorsed and expanded by Gen Walker, who emphasized that the forts were not intended to be passive defensive positions, but rather patrol bases from which the garrison could dominate the area.

The forts varied in strength from platoon to company size, and were built on high ground. Some were accessible by road, but others relied for rations, ammunition and stores on helicopters, short take-off/landing aircraft like the Twin Pioneer or parachute delivery. The packing for parachute drops was a highly developed skill which allowed fragile cargoes like fresh eggs (and even six bottles of champagne to celebrate an officer's birthday) to be delivered safely. There is one unsubstantiated report that a cat was air-dropped to a forward position to assist in anti-rat operations. The drop zone was normally just outside the fort, so that the cargo could be recovered easily but posed no risk to the garrison if there was a parachute malfunction. The parachute material was dyed black and used for lightweight 'zoot suits', which could be worn as an extra layer or for sleeping. Coloured parachute canopies were also attached to trees as 'gun markers' to give artillery a point of reference if fire support was needed (though these were vulnerable to pilfering, as the Ibans favoured them for making clothes).

19

With jungle forts covering more than 900 miles of border and with very few roads, air-dropping of supplies and equipment was vital. Royal Army Service Corps air despatchers (see Plate G3) – who would soon be rebadged to the Royal Corps of Transport – needed quick reactions in the confined space of cargo holds when the doors were opened and heavy parachute loads were being manhandled out over small DZs. Here a crew ready supplies for a parachute delivery as an RAF Hastings transport runs in towards a forward position in Borneo.

RAF fixed-wing transport squadrons deployed were No 215 (with the Argosy C1), 209 (Twin Pioneer CC1), 52 (Valetta C1) & 48 (Hastings C1/2), based at Changi, Butterworth and Selatar with detachments to Labuan and other airfields. The RAAF also contributed its No 36 Sqn (C-130A Hercules); the RNZAF its No 41 Sqn (Bristol 170 Freighters); and the RMAF its No 8 Sqn (Caribous). (IWM FEW 65/60/9)

Like all field defences, the forts used a layered system of obstacles and interlocking fire from automatic weapons. On the perimeter mutually supporting bunkers mounted weapons like the 7.62mm GPMG (General Purpose Machine Gun) or the .303in Vickers medium machine gun. Tunnels or trenches connected the positions; for stocky Gurkhas the trenches were quite shallow, which caused problems if they handed over to a regiment like the Scots Guards, which included many six-footers. The fort would have a watch tower, and communications by telephone line, radio and simple visual signals. Water tanks, latrines and living accommodation would be dug in and sand-bagged.

Each fort had its own 81mm or 3in mortars and one or two 105mm howitzers, which could fire in support of a neighbouring fort or, later, a cross-border patrol. Men of 50 Gurkha Field Engineer Regt and the Royal Engineers built helicopter landing pads as far forward as practicable, in order to reduce dead flying time. Beyond the fort was a belt of mines, barbed wire and *panji* stakes, with trip flares and command-detonated charges such as Claymore mines mixed in; at the furthest limit of visibility was an apron of Dannert wire. Battalions undertook three-to-five month tours in Borneo, and the normal practice was to send a platoon back from its fort to battalion HQ at least once in a tour, to allow the men 'the luxury of sleeping on a bed, however basic, and having a daily shower, however primitive the plumbing'. The reserve platoon at battalion HQ would be ready to reinforce a fort or conduct a follow-up operation, landing or being roped from a helicopter.

1 GJ at Stass, July 1964

In June 1964, patrol bases came under attack as the Indonesians switched their tactics. On the night of 18 July a position at Bukit Knuckle held by 5 Ptn, 1st Bn Green Jackets commanded by Lt Christopher Miers was probed by the enemy. The Riflemen returned fire, and the following morning two pools of blood and splintered bone indicated at least two casualties.

On 31 July a base at Stass manned by 7 Ptn, 1 GJ commanded by 2/Lt Peter Chamberlin came under a night attack. Major M.Koe, commanding B Coy, had anticipated this and had positioned 11 Ptn under 2/Lt Roberts about 1,000 yards south of the base as a cut-off ambush. Roberts positioned remotely-triggered flares, No.36 grenades linked with detonating cord for simultaneous detonation, and *panjis*. At 02.30hrs, Stass came under fire from LMGs and 50mm mortars from a range of about 80 yards. Chamberlin's men returned fire with their 3in mortar and small arms, and 105mm defensive fire fell 150 yards from the platoon perimeter. At 03.00 the Indonesians withdrew under harassing artillery fire. At 04.12, a group of men chattering excitedly entered 11 Ptn's ambush area. Roberts estimated their strength as around 30, moving in single file; they were led by a man with a torch, and the soldiers at point were armed with shotguns. As the last of the Indonesians entered the killing ground Roberts set off the flares. The ambush lasted 15 seconds; the following morning one body was found near 7 Ptn's base and four more in the ambush area, together with blood on the *panjis*. It was later confirmed that an Indonesian regular unit lost a lieutenant, a sergeant and four privates, with five wounded and nine others missing.

2 Para at Plaman Mapu, April 1965
The most ambitious attack on a company base came near the end of the Confontation, at Plaman Mapu in the First Division on 27 April 1965. The position was held by B Coy HQ, 2nd Bn The Parachute Regiment, plus a weak platoon of soldiers fresh from the depot; the bulk of the company was out on patrol. The paratroop battalion had deployed to Borneo only in March. In the position were three officers including Capt Webb, the artillery forward observation officer (FOO); Company Sergeant Major Williams, and cooks, mortar crews and radio operators – a total strength of 34 men. At 04.45hrs, during the usual nighttime downpour, the position came under mortar and rocket-launcher fire. The attackers were from a tough Javanese unit of the Indonesian regular army: the 3rd Bn, Para-Commando Regt (RPKAD), commanded by LtCol Saro Edhie Widabowo. The RPKAD had seen a good deal of action in the 1950s and early 1960s, including several combat jumps; they enjoyed elite status as trusted guards of the regime, and had good equipment from a mixture of sources both Soviet and Western.

The Para-Commandos cut the perimeter wire with Bangalore torpedoes, and launched three assaults. The first gained a lodgement in the position, capturing an 81mm mortar pit. CSM Williams and Capt Thompson, the acting platoon commander, rallied the Paras, but Thompson was wounded by mortar fire. With the situation deteriorating, Williams recalled thinking, 'This is it – this is the end of the story anyway, so I'll give 'em a bit of rapid fire'. He discarded his rifle and grabbed a GPMG, clipped two more belts to that already in the gun, and stood firing from the hip, as Cpl Baughan led a counter-attack. Several of the Indonesians charged straight at Williams, the nearest being killed only two yards away from him.

When the second assault came in, with supporting fire and Bangalore torpedoes, 105mm howitzers were able to fire on the enemy axis of attack. Inside the position, CSM Williams brought another GPMG up, and Sgt McDonald fired the 81mm mortar vertically, using only the primary charge, so that the bombs fell only 30 yards away. This broke up the second assault. The third attack just before dawn, at about 05.45, was not pressed home with great vigour.

When CSM Williams took out a clearing patrol he found one Indonesian, whom he killed. There was no other sign of the enemy, only a wide blood trail littered with discarded equipment and dressings, leading towards the border. B Company had lost two men killed and seven wounded. Enemy weapons recovered included Armalite rifles, some of them M203s incorporating the 40mm grenade launcher; Soviet AK-47 assault rifles and RPD light machine guns. Subsequent intelligence analysis revealed that the Paras had been attacked by two companies supported by 18 Yugoslav-made 44mm M57 rocket

A typical border fort in Sarawak. It has an observation tower, bunkers made of logs and sandbags linked by communication trenches, and a stepped walkway up the hill – essential in the muddy conditions created by tropical rainfall – made of cannibalized ammunition boxes. Note the tall poles supporting radio aerials, and the vegetation cleared away to provide good fields of fire. (IWM FES 64/242/4)

launchers (one of which was captured), eight 50mm mortars and ten machine guns. The Indonesians had suffered about 30 casualties, but there were no bodies. Years later 2 Para's former intelligence officer in 1965 met an Indonesian officer on a course in Britain. The latter told him that the absence of bodies at Plaman Mapu was simply explained: the dead and severely wounded alike had been dumped into a river close to the Indonesian border.

At dawn the battalion medical officer arrived at the position and promptly evacuated CSM Williams; he had been hit by fragments in the side of his head, he was deafened, and he had lost his left eye. The GPMG he had fired had been hit three times, as had the A41 radio in his position. Williams received the Distinguished Conduct Medal for his bravery and leadership that night – a decoration second only to the Victoria Cross in the eyes of British soldiers. The action at Plaman Mapu was later described by FM Lord Carver as 'another defence of Rorke's Drift'.

PATROLLING

From the forts, a company would send out patrols for ten to 15 days of 'jungle bashing', the length dictated by the amount of rations that could be carried by each man. Various patrol techniques were employed, with a platoon aiming to cover a 1,000-metre map square in a day. Among the toughest tasks were river-line patrols, which followed meandering rivers and creeks to locate crossings or water points. The rivers might be fast-flowing between big moss-covered boulders, or slow and swampy. On patrol men would live off cold rations. Food for 24 hours for Gurkhas would consist of a breakfast of tea and 'Biscuits, Plain' (better known as 'dog biscuits'); lunch would be tea, a tin of sardines and dog biscuits; and the evening meal, eaten before last light, would be tea, rice and dried fish. Many of the items in the rations were locally bought rather than part of a British Army 24-hour ration pack. In a patrol report on Operation 'Red River' by 2/2nd GR, the patrol commander said that men carrying weapons, ammunition and 15 days' rations had loads of about 70lbs, while those with the GPMG were carrying nearly 80 pounds.

Tracks were avoided since they might be ambushed or mined, and this could mean hacking through secondary jungle at a rate of about

200 yards an hour. At 17:00hrs, when it would begin to grow dark, it was time to set up a patrol base with simple shelters made from ponchos and parachute cord. By 18.00 the rain would start to fall, often for six hours non stop, while the men attempted to sleep in their wet, muddy uniforms. If the patrol found indications of the enemy, or were following up an enemy attack, the company might bring in a dog team.

SAS tactics – 'shoot and scoot'
Though SAS patrols would ambush the enemy both in Malaysia and later across the border, this was not their primary function. Colonel Woodehouse laid down that the standard operating procedure for a contact would be 'shoot and scoot' – open fire to deter a follow-up, but break off the contact as quickly as possible.

Relieving A Sqn, 22 SAS in May 1963, D Sqn embarked on deep operations along the estuaries in Sarawak's low-lying western frontier region. Tracks over the high ground opposite Long Jawai in the Third Division, the valley south of Pensiangan in southern Sabah, and the coastal estuaries of Sabah were also identified as likely infiltration routes. During their first month D Sqn penetrated a previously unexplored area on the Sabah border known as The Gap; this patrol, commanded by Capt 'Andy' Dennison, included the experienced Sgt Eddie 'Geordie' Lillico. Lillico would later survive an ambush in February 1965 with severe leg wounds, and would crawl for two days, avoiding Indonesian patrols until he reached the helicopter rendezvous.

In the same month, 22 SAS suffered its most serious losses of the campaign when, on 4 May, a Belvedere helicopter crashed on take-off at Ba Kelalan while carrying Maj Ronald Norman, second-in-command of the regiment, the operations officer Maj Harry Thompson, Cpl 'Spud' Murphy and other passengers and crew.

In December 1963, D Sqn completed its first tour and A Sqn returned for a second. During winter 1963–64 Indonesian incursions increased in Sabah; the squadron mounted several long range patrols into Kalimantan, but only close enough to the border that their incursion could be put down to a 'map-reading error'. In March 1964 a patrol commanded by Sgt 'Smokey' Richardson were tasked with covering the border north from Ba Kelanan and meeting a second patrol in a feature known as the Long Pa Sia Bulge. Richardson's patrol confirmed that the Indonesians were crossing the border in strength; they located a large camp, but on the evening of 14 March they 'bumped' a patrol of over a dozen Indonesian soldiers. In a shoot-and-scoot engagement the radio operator, Tpr James 'Paddy' Condon from Tipperary, was wounded in the thigh and became separated; captured by the Indonesians, he was shot after a brief interrogation.

Of the British, Australian and New Zealand SAS patrols, Gen Walker wrote: 'I regard 70 troopers of the SAS as being as valuable to me as 700 infantry in the role of "hearts and minds", border surveillance, early warning, stay-behind, and eyes-and-ears with a sting'.

Men of the Mortar Platoon of 1st Bn Scots Guards in Eastern Brigade, Sabah, 1965. The 81mm mortars are protected by *sangars* made from sandbags, flattened oildrums, corrugated galvanized iron and 6ft angle-iron pickets. Note the AR15 rifles lying on the parapets. The Guardsmen wear basic 44 Ptn belt order with ammo pouches and two waterbottles. One company of 1st Irish Guards served under command of 1 SG, and the Guards Independent Parachute Coy also deployed to Borneo. (1 SG via John Norris)

'CLARET' OPERATIONS

In 1964 Harold Wilson won the General Election and Britain had a Labour government. The Secretary of State for Defence was Dennis Healey, who in World War II had served in the Royal Engineers, rising to the rank of major and seeing action in Italy. The government was committed to supporting the new Commonwealth nations; the threat from Indonesia was evident, and the government was prepared to take tough decisions. Healey and Wilson proved shrewd political allies for Malaysia and for Gen Walker, who was able to convince them of the need for top secret cross-border raids against Indonesian staging camps.

These operations were codenamed 'Claret', and were intended 'to pre-empt any likely build-up or attack, to harass by ambush and patrols the Indonesians, and to induce them to move their camps... away from the border'. Indonesia and the Federation of Malaysia, let alone the United Kingdom, were not officially at war, so it was a risky political move. One British officer serving with Malaysian Rangers recalled the grim preamble to the orders group prior to a Claret operation: 'This operation is deniable and will be denied'. Once the soldiers had crossed the ill-defined jungle border into Indonesia they were on their own. When it was necessary to report the result of a Claret raid to the media, it was described as 'a successful action in the border area'.

The SAS had in fact been crossing the Kalimantan border since December 1963; but now attacks would be undertaken at platoon or even company strength by regular British infantry battalions, working on intelligence gathered by SAS patrols – who also mounted small scale ambushes. A special war room was set up to handle the clandestine operations, which were conducted under strict guidelines known as The Golden Rules:

(1) All raids had to be authorized by the Director of Operations.
(2) Only tried and tested troops were to be used (no soldiers on their first tour of duty in Borneo).
(3) Raids were to be made with the definite aim of deterring and thwarting aggression by the Indonesians. No attacks were to be mounted in retribution or simply with the general aim of inflicting casualties.
(4) Close air support would not be given except in an extreme emergency.

It was emphasized, wrote Brig E.D. 'Birdie' Smith of the Gurkhas, that 'minimum force was to be the principle used, rather than large scale attacks which would have incited retaliation and risked escalation, turning the border war into something quite different, costly in lives and fraught with international problems'.

The first target was the Indonesian garrison at Nantakor south of Pensiangan. The village was within the 3,000m from the border which was at that date the limit allowed, and its defences had been studied by the SAS and Border Scouts, who had located the minefields and crew-served weapons. The troops for the task were A Coy, 1/2nd Gurkhas commanded by Maj Digby Willoughby. The assault went as planned; the Indonesian commander and five of his men were killed and the camp destroyed, at a cost of four Gurkhas wounded.

The Royal Marines of 40 Cdo and the SBS Tawau Assault Group were given an unusual Claret mission on 8 December 1964: they were tasked

(continued on page 33)

1: TNKU officer, North Borneo, December 1962
2: Sgt, Indonesian AF paratroops, 1964
3: NCO, Indonesian Army 328 Para-Raider Bn; Kling-Kang Mts, March 1964

A

1: Private, A Coy, 1st Bn Queen's Own Highlanders; Brunei, December 1962
2: Marine, 42 Cdo RM; Brunei, winter 1962/63
3: Rifleman, 1st Bn Green Jackets; N.Borneo, winter 1962/63

1: NCO, 3rd Bn Royal Australian Regt; Sarawak, June 1965
2: Guardsman, 1st Bn Scots Guards; boat patrol, Sabah, 1964
3: Radio operator, 1st Bn Royal Ulster Rifles; Sarawak, July 1964

1: Trooper, D Sqn, 22nd SAS Regt, 1963
2: Dog handler, 2nd Bn Green Jackets, 1965
3: Punan tracker, 1963

1: Lance-Naik Rambahadur Limbu (VC), C Coy, 2nd Bn, 10th Gurkha Rifles; Gunong Tepoi, 21 November 1965
2: Rifleman, 1st Bn, 10th Gurkha Rifles; Labis, September 1964
3: Lt, 2nd Bn, 7nd Gurkha Rifles; Lumbis, June 1965

E

1: WO2, Royal Army Pay Corps
2: Sergeant, Royal Army Medical Corps
3: Vice-Admiral, RN
4: Captain, Queen's Royal Irish Hussars

1: Petty Officer, RN landing party, 1964
2: Sgt helicopter pilot, 656 Sqn AAC
3: L/Cpl, 15 Air Despatch Regt, RASC; Kuching, 1964

G

1: CSM, B Coy, 2nd Bn The Parachute Regt;
   Plaman Mapu, 27 April 1965
2: Iban Border Scout, 2nd Bn 10th Gurkha Rifles, 1965

H

with neutralizing an Indonesian observation post on Sebatik Island off Sabah's east coast, which was close to an Indonesian base on Nanukan Island. In an earlier century the Dutch and British colonial cartographers had divided Sebatik, an island measuring about 25 by 12 miles, almost exactly in half: the southern portion was now Indonesian and the northern was part of Sabah. The SBS had reconnoitred the OP earlier in 1964; and on 8 December the motor cruiser *Bob Sawyer* carried a group of Royal Marines under command of an SBS officer, Lt R.A.M.Seeger, to a point off the coast. Here they launched three Gemini inflatables; one carried a support party with a GPMG to a position on the border, to deter any Indonesian pursuit after the attack. The other two boats, with 15 men aboard, paddled the 6 miles to a small beach. Seeger had divided the 15 men into a GPMG crew under Sgt Costley, a close quarter assault group with Sterling SMGs under Cpl Tomlin, and two scouts with Armalites fitted with electric torches.

As the two inflatables reached the shore the Indonesians opened inaccurate fire. The Royal Marines put in a quick assault with supporting fire from the GPMG on the beach. Ranges were so close that when Seeger shouted 'Grenade!' and threw two into the observation post, the GPMG crew held the gun above their heads and ducked under water to avoid the blast. Seeger raked the building with fire, and in the light of the campfire the Marines spotted three bodies; but, with orders not to be drawn into a sustained firefight, they then withdrew. Soon afterwards the Indonesians began to mortar the area of the OP, but by then the SBS were out of danger.

This was not the only Claret operation led by Lt Seeger, who had already undertaken two reconnaissance patrols in October 1964. On 12 September 1965, firing at ranges of about 40 yards during Operation 'Freefall', D Coy of 40 Cdo expended over 900 rounds of 7.62mm, 200 rounds of 9mm, 100 rounds of 5.56m and eight grenades; the attack, initiated by Seeger with his Armalite, was described crisply as 'a good operation'.

On 30 November 1965, in Operation 'James Bond', 130 men of the 2/2nd Gurkha Rifles fought off four enemy attacks in company strength inside Indonesia. Contacts, like most in the jungle, were at five yards' range, and men could describe their adversaries in considerable detail. The enemy wore 'OG uniforms, with pale

A patrol from 2 GJ move out through the outer wire perimeter of their fort in 1965; the Rifleman in the foreground has a 30-round LMG magazine on his SLR. The Tiger Beer cans tied to the barbed wire contain pebbles, which rattled if an intruder tried to cut his way through the defences at night. (IWM FEW 65/32/42)

green flashes on the sleeves. They wore jungle hats, some turned up on both sides and one had a red flash on the left side. One man had a white chevron on the left sleeve'. With this level of observation by his soldiers, Capt Erskine-Tulloch could have confidence in his report of 24 confirmed enemy dead and ten wounded.

Some Claret operations were on a large scale, such as that in mid May 1966 when both L & M Coys of 42 Cdo RM crossed the border south of Biawak in Sarawak's First Division. A two-day march with an over-night harbour brought them close to an Indonesian base. Their final approach to the target was at night – no easy task in the jungle, with nearly 200 men. Once they were in position around the *kampong* Claymore mines attached to bamboo poles were positioned to fire downwards through the roofs of the huts. At dawn the mines were detonated and the attack was sprung with GPMGs and Armalites. The only Royal Marine casualty was Capt Ian Clark, who died of his wounds.

Riflemen of 2nd Green Jackets about to set out on a five-day patrol on the jungle border between Sarawak and Kalimantan. The patrol commander makes a last-minute check of arms and equipment; once out on patrol their only contact with their base will be by radio, and even a small item of equipment left behind could mean that the mission will not be accomplished. They wear 44 Ptn equipment with poncho rolls strapped to the haversack, and the patrol commander has a 'gollock' machete at his hip. Apart from 1 & 2 GJ and 2 Para, English and Irish line battalions which deployed to the Far East at various dates were as follows (1st Bns in each case): Royal Leicesters, Royal Ulster Rifles, Queen's Own Buffs, Durham Light Infantry, Royal Warwickshire Fusiliers, Royal Hampshires and King's Own Yorkshire Light Infantry. (IWM FEW 65/32/34)

SAS CLARET OPERATIONS

In the winter of 1964–65, A & B Sqns, 22 SAS conducted a number of cross-border operations; patrols from B Sqn were concentrated on the Puch range of hills in western Sarawak, intercepting agents attempting to contact CCO cells in Lundu. Early in 1965, D Sqn under Maj Roger Woodiwiss replaced A Sqn again, and the Claret operations continued. In April a four-man patrol led by Capt Robin Letts near Babang Baba in Kalimantan monitored Indonesian traffic on the Sentimo river, and on the morning of the 28th they sprung an ambush against two longboats. In four minutes, at ranges as close as 8ft, they killed five Indonesian soldiers; one escaped.

In May 1965, Maj Woodiwiss briefed Sgt Don 'Lofty' Large – formerly of the Gloucestershire Regt, and a veteran of the Korean War – to lead a patrol across the border to the Koemba river near Poeri. On 10 May they encountered an Indonesian platoon, but carefully skirted their position. When they had located a position for an OP on the edge of a rubber plantation they watched the river traffic. The following day a 45ft luxury motor yacht appeared. 'At the stern was the red and white flag... only those boats with soldiers on board had flown it so far. Amidships a... canopy shaded its occupants so that Large could not make them out. On a short mast... flew another banner, this one having a strange device that strongly suggested to his practised eye the sort which very senior officers display to boost their egos and inspire awe. "We'll have this one", Large whispered.' It was then that he saw a young girl among the passengers. Wondering if this meant that the boat carried a civilian official, they let it pass; and 12 years later, Gen Moerdani of the Indonesian Parachute Regt had an opportunity to thank two former members of the patrol for their chivalry. Large had been right: the flag had been the guidon of the then Col Moerdani.

It took another day before another target presented itself; then, in driving rain, the patrol opened fire at 45 yards' range on a 40ft launch with two soldiers at the stern and a deck cargo under tarpaulins. Hit by more than 60 rounds, the boat took on a list and started to burn, and the smell of burning fuel borne on the wind followed the patrol as they withdrew.

In late May 1965, D Sqn was replaced by A Sqn, commanded by Maj Peter de la Billiere. That August, working closely with the Gurkhas, the squadron launched a series of cross-border raids. Many were fruitless; during an operation in September, 12 four-man patrols conducted a vain three-week search for a reported CCO camp on the headwaters of the Sempayang and Bemban rivers on Sarawak's western border.

In December 1965 the new Director of Operations, MajGen George Lea, cleared 6, 7 & 8 Tps of B Sqn for an extensive spread of ambushes on the Bemban-to-Sawah track. The Indonesians had been alerted by two locals, but when they attempted to roll up one ambush in a series of fire-and-manoeuvre moves, five were caught in the blast of a Claymore: 'The result was shocking... hats, limbs, bodies flew and then lay grotesquely still... The remaining two Claymores pointing down the track were fired blind and produced screams and groans, evidently from a follow-up force which must have been halted in its tracks, for it never appeared.' Among the ambushers on this occasion was Tpr John White, whose brother Billy had been killed in an ambush while serving with A Sqn in August 1964. John White had been so impressed when he attended his brother's memorial service at Hereford that he had volunteered for the Regiment.

An interesting development from this period was the formation, at the close of the campaign in 1966, of G (for Guards) Sqn, 22 SAS. The squadron was composed of men from the disbanded Guards Independent Parachute Company, which had undertaken patrolling and close reconnaissance missions on the central Sarawak border. Commanded by Maj L.G.S.Head, the company had come to Borneo in June 1964, and conducted its first Claret operations in September 1965.

Australian SAS

From February to July 1965, 1 Sqn, Australian Special Air Service Regiment served in Brunei, and 2 Sqn from February to July 1966 in Sarawak; they suffered three killed in action.

Brigadier Harry Tuzo, commander of the Central Brigade where they operated, noted that the Australians 'appeared to be extremely keen and tough and are to operate on the same lines as the British SAS'. No.1 Squadron's commander, Maj Alf Garland, flew in with an advanced party on 16 February and was briefed about the 'Golden Rules', laid down in 1964 but eased a year later. In *SAS Phantoms of the Jungle,* David Horner spells out these rules in greater detail than the other accounts, and the final paragraphs give an indication of how sensitive these operations were thought to be:

'Every operation must be planned with the aid of a sand-table and thoroughly rehearsed for at least two weeks. Each operation to be planned and executed with maximum security. Every man taking part must be sworn to secrecy, full cover plans must be made and the operations to be given code-names and never discussed in detail on

A hazard of long jungle patrols – the rubber sole of the jungle boot has parted from the canvas upper. These light boots were comfortable but not robust enough for the conditions, and needed replacing frequently. (Author's collection)

telephones or radio. Identity discs must be left behind before departure and no traces – such as cartridge cases, paper ration packs, etc – must be left in Kalimantan. On no account must any soldier taking part be captured by the enemy – alive or dead.'

Although the squadron had adopted the sand-coloured beret of the British SAS these had not yet been issued, and the men arrived in Singapore wearing their red berets. A day later, Radio Djakarta announced that the British Parachute Regiment had deployed to the theatre.

Four-man patrols normally lasted about two weeks. They would be flown into the area by fixed wing aircraft, lifted to the border by helicopter, and then might rope down into the jungle. They carried Bergens weighing nearly 90lb – almost twice the weight recommended in SOPs. Some rations would be cached to be recovered on the return leg of the patrol. Each man had a coloured identification band sewn to the inside of his jungle hat; when he was approaching friendly forces the hat would be worn inside out, showing the colour. The belt order had ammunition pouches with 60 rounds of 7.62mm or 100 of 5.56mm, and water bottles. An emergency pack held rations, tetracycline and salt tablets, and an air marker panel. A compass was attached to the neck by a lanyard.

Within the patrol, communications were either by whispers or hand signals. The radio operator sent a coded message every 24 hours at a scheduled time; if the radio malfunctioned or the schedules could not be met the patrol would activate its SARBE (search and rescue beacon) at set times, or when an aircraft was in the vicinity. Each patrol had a codeword which meant 'I am being chased and am heading for the Border (or Exfiltration) RV'; if this signal was heard, a helicopter would home in on the SARBE.

The second Claret operation on 2 May 1965 was commanded by Lt Tom Marshall, a former ranker, who enforced weight discipline on his three men: each soldier carried only 30lb of equipment, in one 44 Ptn and three wicker basket packs. Breakfast and the midday snack were both half a bar of chocolate or half a packet of raisins and a brew of tea; the main meal was a tin of meat and vegetables, and tea. The diet was improved by wild fruit, and the men took vitamin tablets. The patrol was out for 12 days; when it returned each man had lost between 6lbs and 10lbs – but they had set up an OP overlooking Labang in Indonesia, and observed 15 enemy in two huts.

Reconnaissance patrols continued, and the first offensive Claret operation by the Australian SAS, against Lumbis, took place in June 1965. Corporal Robinson guided B Coy, 2/7th Gurkhas with GPMGs and 81mm mortars into position on the wet night of 25 June. The ambush was sprung at 09.00 when the Indonesians began their morning meal; 50 minutes later the order to withdraw was given, and as the

A Royal Marine section grouped around their Bedford 3 ton truck after returning from a 'Claret' operation inside Kalimantan. The first Claret operations penetrated only up to 3,000m (3,270 yards) inside Indonesian territory; but in 1964 MajGen Walker's units were authorized to extend this to 10,000m (c.11,000 yards – over 6 miles), and raids were eventually pushing 20,000m (nearly 11 miles) into Indonesia. By 1965 British dominance of the jungle meant that almost all infantry operations were of this type. (RM Museum)

Australians and Gurkhas pulled back 105mm howitzers at Kabu shelled the *kampong*. A week later a Border Scout visited the area and reported that the Indonesians were 'very much afraid'.

One patrol led by Sgt John Pettit had been observing the Salirir river east of Baluladan since 3 July, when at 17.00 on the 5th they saw a boat with nine men, only one of whom was wearing an olive drab shirt, trousers and cap; the cargo included what appeared to be an ammunition box. Pettit sprung the ambush when the boat was 10 yards away; his patrol fired 81 rounds of 7.62mm and 26 rounds of 9mm, and he estimated that they had killed seven and seriously wounded two. Subsequent reports from local civilians via the Border Scouts stated that five soldiers had been killed including a sergeant-major, and two more had died later from wounds.

On 21 July, a large fighting patrol led by 2/Lt Trevor Roderick was watching river traffic when, just after midday, they saw a narrowboat with an outboard motor and six men in white T-shirts and blue shorts. There was no obvious indication that they were soldiers, but the sharp eyes of the Bren gunner, L/Cpl Chris Jennison, spotted kit bags, rifles and webbing at the bottom of the boat; he opened fire, with his officer acting as No.2 on the gun. A total of 60 rounds were fired by two Brens and 52 by the eight SLRs; all six Indonesians were killed.

During its deployment 1 Sqn, SASR spent three months on Claret operations, and killed 17 enemy for the loss of one trooper – Paul Dennehey, who was fatally injured not by Indonesian fire but by a rogue elephant, during an operation in May 1965.

New Zealand SAS

In February 1965, 40 men of the New Zealand SAS commanded by Maj W.J.D.Meldrum arrived in Borneo to take over some of the work. The Kiwis spent a month training at Tutong in Brunei; skills learned and improved included 'hot contact' drills involving fast, close range shooting, as well as navigation and survival. They then moved to Kuching in western Sarawak, where they were attached to 22 SAS. In August 1965, 2 Detachment NZSAS, under Maj R.S.Bearing, arrived in Singapore and, after training at Tutong, moved to Kuching to replace 1 Det on 6 October.

In the First and Second Division areas the NZSAS took their turn at monitoring river traffic inside Indonesia. W.D.Baker took part in one patrol which found a good observation and ambush position, with a clear field of fire and good routes in and out. The day passed quietly, until they saw a longboat with outboard motor struggling upstream heavily laden with stores, and crewed by alert, armed Indonesian soldiers. It was photographed by the patrol commander, who debriefed his men about what had they seen; they had recognized Armalites, and were convinced that the boat was on a supply run to an Indonesian camp upstream. They decided to ambush it on its return, and about two hours later the sound of an outboard motor alerted them.

Men of 1st Scots Guards in a Mk 4 Assault Boat on a watercourse in Sabah's East Brigade; a light machine gun is mounted in the bow. The jungle rivers were necessarily used by both sides as major transport arteries, and many Claret operations involved observation and ambushes of Indonesian river traffic. (1 SG via John Norris)

When the boat entered the 'A' point of the ambush – the point where the coxswain would be unable to turn it – the troopers opened fire, and the ambush was over in seconds; four Indonesians were killed and two wounded.

In July 1966, 4 Det NZSAS under Maj D.W.S.Moloney arrived in theatre. Their tour included a contact with Indonesian troops as late as 5 August; the NZSAS patrol, led by the appositely named Lt 'Alby' Kiwi, followed the Indonesians, who were north of the border. On 12 August, while they were still in the jungle, the Federation of Malaysia and Indonesia signed a peace agreement.

THE LAST YEAR

During 1965 there were confused political signals from Djakarta, and it was therefore felt to be politically expedient to reduce the cross-border pressure. The British soldiers nicknamed these periods 'Be kind to Indos', and in reality they allowed the Indonesians to regroup for what would be the final spasms of the campaign.

On the Malaysian side of the border, following the action at the 2 Para fort at Plaman Mapu in April, the Paras had further contacts with the Indonesians on 15 May 1965 near the village of Mongkus. Men of 10 Ptn outflanked an ambush where about 100 Indonesians were covering a track junction; for the loss of one man the Paras killed five and drove off the enemy force. In a follow-up after dark an Iban tracker literally used his hands to feel out the route, until by 02.00 they were so close that they could smell the enemy, but by dawn the Indonesians had slipped away; artillery fire was called down on their likely routes.

On 22 May a helicopter assault put seven platoons of 2 Para into an area between Mongkus and Mujat to cover the likely route of 50 Indonesians. Before the Paras roped down the area had been prepared by artillery fire and armed helicopters. It fell to a section commander, Cpl Tindale of 10 Ptn, to make contact. He heard movement, set his section up in a snap ambush, and when about 40 Indonesians broke cover on a ridge he waited until they were only 20ft away before he gave the order to fire. The two Bren guns and the section's SLRs killed 14 enemy, and when the Indonesians began to mortar the position and roll it up from the flank Tindale withdrew his little force without suffering any casualties.

Gunong Tepoi: Rambahadur Limbu, VC

On 21 November 1965, on the Indonesian side of the border west of Bau in the extreme west of Sarawak's First Division, L/Naik (L/Cpl) Rambahadur Limbu of the 2/10th Gurkha Rifles won the only Victoria Cross of the campaign. The action was one of two Claret operations by the 2/10th, while the 2/2nd made four attacks, and B Sqn, 22 SAS launched cross-border attacks in near squadron strength, killing 20 Indonesians.

In Operation 'Time Keeper', C Coy, 2/10th GR commanded by Capt Maunsell, reinforced by HQ Coy's Recce and Assault Pioneer platoons, had approached the area of an Indonesian platoon position, and a close reconnaissance by Lt Ranjit Rai of 7 Ptn had located it. The entrenched camp was about 3 miles across the border, at the apex of three knife-edged ridges forming an isolated hill, Gunong Tepoi; the two eastern ridges were covered in thick secondary jungle, as were the deep surrounding valleys. On the morning of 20 November, Capt Maunsell and Lt Bhagat Bahadur Rai of 8 Ptn moved close to the objective and examined it in detail; the camp was still under construction, with fatigue parties at work. About 500 yards beyond it on lower, cultivated ground was a company-strength Indonesian position with mortars, in the hamlet of Babang. The secondary jungle was a serious barrier, almost as effective as barbed wire.

On the morning of the 21st the company moved off, and 800 yards from the target they paused and ate a silent meal of cold rations; then, leaving the Assault Pioneer Ptn securing the patrol base, the company advanced west in the order 7, 8, Recce and 9 Platoons. Maunsell and three Gurkhas cut a 400-yard tunnel through the secondary jungle using gardeners' secateurs for silence. By 13.30 they were creeping north up the southern ridge and were only 20 yards from the Indonesians; the final obstacles were two rows of felled trees which blocked the two-yard wide ridgetop. As they crossed the second obstacle an Indonesian soldier appeared; he unslung his rifle, and was shot. Racing along the ridge four abreast, the Gurkhas attacked immediately, 7 Ptn leading on the left; Lt Ranjit grenaded a machine gun post which had delayed them, and 8 Ptn swung to the right, but moments later heavy fire again stalled the attack. Captain Maunsell crawled forward to recover a wounded Gurkha and, firing from the hip, Lt Bhagat led another rush by 8 Ptn which took them into the enemy trenches.

On the left flank, L/Cpl Rambahadur Limbu of 7 Ptn led a Bren gun crew to silence an enemy machine gun. He sprinted under fire through the open vegetation and neutralized the position with grenades, but his two-man gun crew were wounded by small arms fire and, unable to move, took cover near a prominent tree. Unable to report this development to his platoon commander, Lt Ranjit, under heavy fire Rambahadur decided to bring his friends into cover. Over a period of 20 minutes he dodged small arms fire to make two dashes to pick up the two men, and carried them back to safety one by one – a distance of about 70 yards, four times in succession. Sadly, when they were under cover it was discovered that both of them were dead.

After twice risking his life for his comrades, the Gurkha corporal now realized that their LMG was lying abandoned in an Indonesian trench. He again ran forward under fire; and when he had picked up the gun

Near Bario, Sarawak, 23 May 1966: Gurkhas prepare to board a FAA Wessex on a typically cramped jungle LZ. The jungle offered few natural landing zones for helicopters. Platforms of logs and tamped earth were constructed near forward positions, often on small rises from which the vegetation had been cleared, which allowed the pilot an unrestricted approach. On operations small patrols would rope down from the helicopter into tiny gaps in the canopy, but larger forces would be landed in clearings or on the shingle banks of rivers. The Wessex could carry up to 16 troops.
Naval Air Squadrons deployed to various locations ashore from the commando carriers HMS *Albion* and *Bulwark* were Nos 845, 846, 847 & 848 NAS. (Royal Navy)

he launched an attack on two Indonesian machine gun positions. Charging across the hilltop supported by a section from 7 Ptn, he put the guns out of action and personally killed at least four Indonesians. Captain Maunsell wrote of Rambahadur, 'That he was able to achieve what he did without being hit was miraculous. His outstanding personal bravery, selfless conduct, complete contempt of the enemy and his determination to save the lives of the men of his fire group set an incomparable example and inspired all who saw him'.

It took a final right flanking assault to secure the position, and then Maunsell awaited the expected counter-attack. There was initially some firing in the direction of 9 Ptn, and though the enemy were unseen the smoke from their weapons provided an adequate target location; when Cpl Krishnabahadur Rai fired 150 rounds from his GPMG at the area, the firing ceased. Lieutenant Bhuwansing Limbu spread his Recce Ptn along the approach ridge on the right of 9 Platoon. When two Indonesian soldiers appeared, followed by three more, they were hit by a broadside of fire from this fire support group. When Indonesian light mortars opened fire the Gurkhas replied with their 2in tubes, which must have been on target, because the firing ceased. A textbook counter-attack by six Indonesians using fire and movement was stopped when three men rose to make a forward bound and were again met by a storm of fire from the Gurkhas.

Finally, the Indonesian company position at Babang put in an attack with about 70 men, and Maunsell called for ten rounds of artillery fire

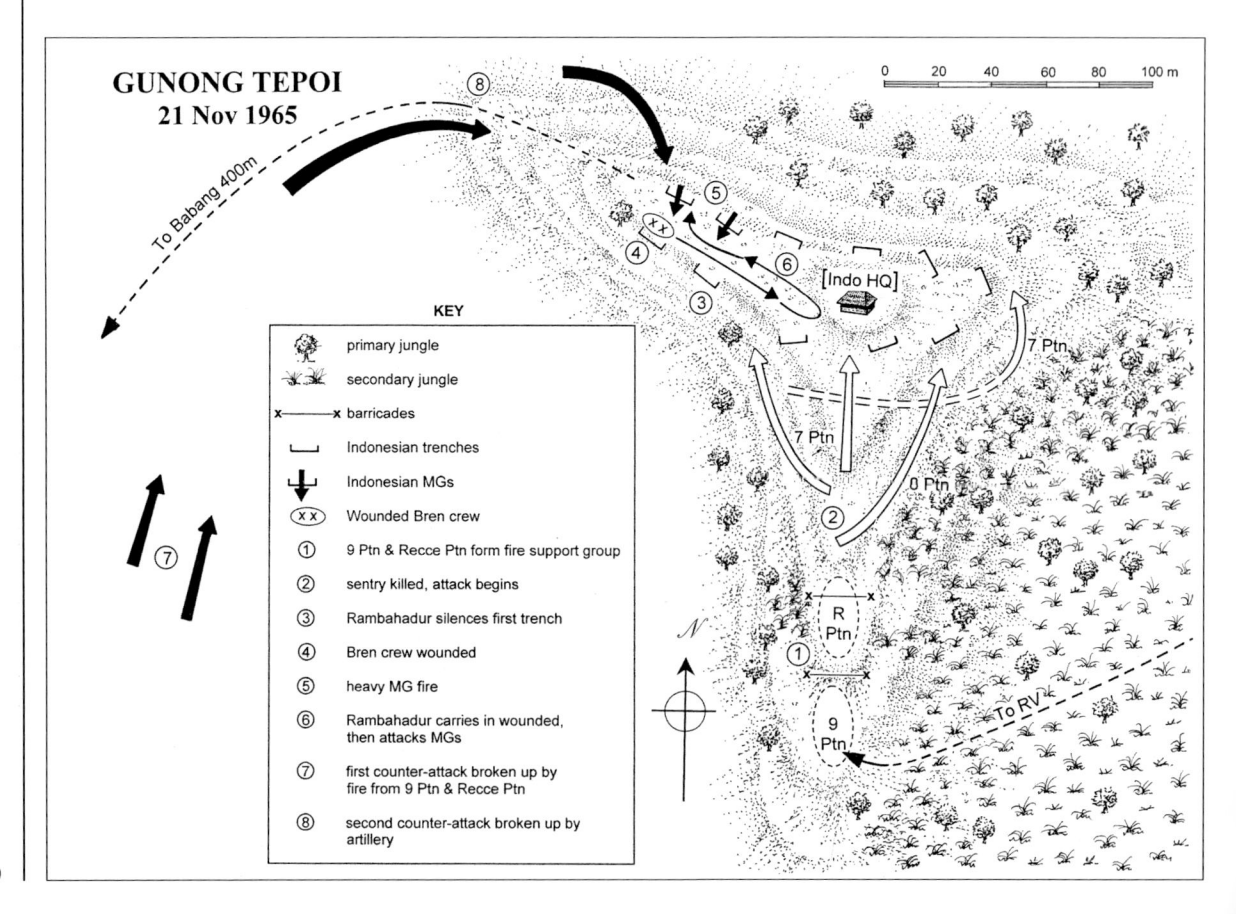

GUNONG TEPOI
21 Nov 1965

KEY
- primary jungle
- secondary jungle
- x——x barricades
- Indonesian trenches
- Indonesian MGs
- xx Wounded Bren crew
- ① 9 Ptn & Recce Ptn form fire support group
- ② sentry killed, attack begins
- ③ Rambahadur silences first trench
- ④ Bren crew wounded
- ⑤ heavy MG fire
- ⑥ Rambahadur carries in wounded, then attacks MGs
- ⑦ first counter-attack broken up by fire from 9 Ptn & Recce Ptn
- ⑧ second counter-attack broken up by artillery

from his FOO. The first salvo almost landed on the Gurkhas, with a chunk of metal slicing into a tree only a few feet from Maunsell's head. The gunners corrected their fire, and the next salvo crashed into the scrub among the Indonesians. Maunsell had neutralized the position, and his company had killed at least 24 of the enemy, so he now gave the order to withdraw to their rendezvous. Once the Gurkhas were clear – taking with them their three dead, one seriously and one lightly wounded – Maunsell called down a barrage of 5.5in and 105mm fire on the vacated position. The action had lasted about 90 minutes.

Captain Maunsell and Lt Ranjit Rai each received the Military Cross, and L/Cpl Rambahadur Limbu was awarded the Victoria Cross. His citation stated that he had displayed 'heroism, self-sacrifice and a devotion to duty and to his men of the very highest order. His actions on this day reached a zenith of determined, premeditated valour which must count among the most notable on record'. Ironically, because Claret operations were secret, the location of the Gunong Tepoi action had to be concealed; it was described as being in the Bau district inside Sarawak. To the uninformed this made the Indonesians appear much more aggressive and effective than they really were, apparently capable of penetrating across the border in strength and building a company position in the jungle; in reality, they had been pushed onto the defensive by the Claret operations.

Getting out

By late 1965 it was clear to the Indonesian armed forces that they were losing the Confrontation, and – like the Argentine defeat in the Falklands campaign in 1982 – this triggered dissension at home. President Sukarno had flirted with the CCO, and the domestic Indonesian Communist Party (PKI) also enjoyed his patronage, which aroused suspicion among the strongly anti-communist military. On 1 October 1965 the PKI launched a coup, killing six generals; among those who escaped were Gen Suharto, a future leader of Indonesia, and Gen Nasution, an influential former defence minister. The Army then led an anti-communist purge over several months during which more than 250,000 PKI members were massacred. On 21 February 1966, Sukarno attempted to reduce the authority of his generals, but on 11 March he was forced to sign an order handing all executive power to Gen Suharto. The Army then moved swiftly to bring an end to Confrontation, which was reckoned to be consuming about 60 per cent of all government expenditure.

At the end of 1965 the number of British troops in Borneo had been reduced from a campaign peak of 17,000 to 14,000. By March 1966 the Confrontation had effectively ended; a provisional agreement signed in Bangkok on 1 June was ratified in Djakarta on 11 August 1966. The Indonesians sent a military mission to the Malaysian capital, Kuala Lumpur, headed by Col Moerdani – the paratroop officer who had been spared by SAS Sgt 'Lofty' Large during a Claret operation.

The Confrontation had cost the Commonwealth military and civilian services 150 dead, 234 wounded and 4 captured; of this total the British

Rambahadur Limbu, VC, 2/10th Gurkha Rifles (see Plate E1), photographed later as a Havildar (sergeant). He went on to be commissioned, and to serve out a long and distinguished career as a Gurkha officer.
Although a very few posthumous awards were made during later 20th century campaigns, Limbu was the only British soldier who survived to be decorated with the Victoria Cross between 1965, and the award to Pte Johnson Beharry of 1st Bn Princess of Wales's Royal Regt for gallantry in Iraq in May and June 2004. (Gurkha Welfare Trust)

suffered 19 killed and 44 wounded, and the Gurkhas, who had borne the brunt of the Claret raids, 40 killed and 83 wounded. The Indonesians suffered 590 dead, 222 wounded and 771 captured. The British Prime Minister Harold Wilson, Defence Minister Dennis Healey and Gens Walter Walker and George Lea had ensured that this undeclared war remained a 'low intensity operation' – the Indonesians were kept under pressure, but never publicly provoked or humiliated in a way that might have escalated or prolonged the war.

* * *

In Vietnam the US forces were facing a far stronger and more committed enemy and, in their rear areas, highly organized guerrillas. On a heavily populated battlefield their massive firepower caused heavy civilian casualties, with inevitable consequences. The British and Commonwealth troops deployed to Malaysia were spared a comparable ordeal. Infantry warfare deep in the Borneo jungle was terribly punishing; the death of close comrades is as shockingly painful for soldiers whether the total casualties amount to a few hundred or tens of thousands, and as devastating for their families at home.[3] However, the Confrontation was very largely a soldiers' war, and relationships with the local populations were usually easy-going. For many British, Australian and New Zealand veterans there were some happier memories of the Confrontation: they recall the beer, the girls and the songs.

The beer was Carlsberg from Denmark, locally produced Anchor, or Tiger – an excellent lager brewed in Singapore. The girls were part of the exotic Oriental nightlife enjoyed by soldiers who had been amassing pay while serving on the border. For some young soldiers, however, encounters with the seductive charms of the *kaitais* of Bugis Street, Singapore, taught them that while external appearances could be delightful, closer acquaintance revealed some startling surprises.

The songs were the pop hits of the early 1960s, among them a number by the British group The Animals which was sung by the soldiers with ironic gusto: *'We've gotta get out of this place, if it's the last thing we ever do...'* Within a couple of years, about 1,000 miles to the north across the South China Sea, US servicemen would be singing the same chorus with similar enthusiasm as the sign-off number to USO shows in the jungles of Vietnam.

At Gunong Tepoi the FOO, Lt Fox RA, was able to call down artillery fire from bases inside Sarawak to cover the withdrawal of Capt Maunsell's Gurkhas. There were two 105mm pack howitzers at C Coy's main base camp at Serikin, about 5 1/2 miles to the east, and a single 5.5in gun at Pejiru, about twice as far north-east. This photo shows one of the Italian-designed Oto Melara M56 105mm pack howitzers of F Tp, 176 Bty RA at gun practice in a forward position in Sarawak during 1964; note the white square recognition signs on the front and back of the crew's jungle hats. Royal Artillery elements deployed during the campaign were all or some batteries of the following regiments: 4, 6, 40 & 45 Light; 29 & 95 Commando Light; 12, 16 & 22 Light Air Defence; 20 Medium; 94 Locating; plus Locating Tp, 3 RHA, and Air OP Tp, 49 Field Regiment. (IWM FES 64/243/3)

3 Simply as an example: Capt Ian Clark of 42 Cdo RM, killed so late in the conflict, was a family friend of the editor of this series. He left a widowed bride of less than a year, carrying the child he never saw.

THE PLATES

Additional material by Nick van der Bijl

A1: TNKU officer, North Borneo, December 1962

The *Tentara Nasional Kalimantan Utara* produced a home-made uniform with rudimentary insignia. This figure is based on a khaki shirt in the RM Museum; a second is green, bearing only the chest patch, 'TNKU' shoulder titles, and broad dark green outer loops on the shoulder straps. A blue example captured by 1 GJ, said to be that of the 'Blue Platoon' based at Lawas in Sarawak, bears plain white shoulder strap loops but all the other insignia illustrated here, including the right sleeve patch; this shows a yellow sun above three stars between the horns of a black buffalo head, on a white background. Despite the obvious effort to establish the TNKU on 'regular' lines with ranks and insignia, some members wore civilian shorts or sarongs and 'flip-flop' sandals, and there was no specific headdress. Many carried the 12-bore shotguns which were widely used for hunting, but with single-slug cartridges for combat.

A2: Sergeant, Indonesian Air Force paratroops (PGT), 1964

Indonesia's original airborne unit – tracing their lineage to a handful of anti-Dutch guerrillas who jumped into Kalimantan in October 1949 – the *Pasukan Gerak Tjepat* or Fast Mobile Force saw action in the 1950s–60s against anti-government rebels, before being committed to both airborne and seaborne insertions during the Confrontation in 1964. By the next year the PGT had three battalions, headquartered at Bandung; the force was later redesignated KOPASGAT, and finally PASHKAS – Air Force Special Forces – in 1983. Photos taken during the 1960s show this one-piece camouflage overall based on the US M1942 jungle suit with four external pockets. The squashed-looking field cap in drab herringbone twill seems to have been common (the orange beret of KOPASGAT was not yet used). The insignia worn here on barracks dress were not displayed in the field: the Air Force Special Forces left shoulder patch **(inset A4)**, the PGT title in black on yellow on the right breast, and yellow metal Air Force parachute wings on the left. Rank was Dutch style, worn on shoulder strap slides. In the field, webbing equipment was of US M1956 pattern, and the standard personal weapon was the 7.62mm NATO FN-FAL rifle.

A3: NCO, 328 Para-Raider Battalion, Indonesian Army; Kling-Kang Mountains, March 1964

On 7 March 1964 a company of this unit was intercepted by 2/10th GR on Track 6 in the Kling-Kang range, and much equipment and intelligence material was captured, including photos upon which this figure is based. The field cap and uniform are in the same camouflage pattern as that worn by A2, but the suit is two-piece and lacks the large thigh pockets. Webbing comprises a US M1956 pistol belt and suspenders, with double clip pouches for his M1 carbine and holstered Colt M1911A1 – the latter being the only sign of his NCO status. The US M3 'grease gun' SMG was also carried by this unit. There were several versions of the Raider right sleeve patch; the example shown **(inset A5)** is believed to be contemporary.

These Army airborne infantry units should not be confused with the Para-Commando Regt (RPKAD), which was also

Saladins of the Queen's Royal Irish Hussars pause while on patrol during the Brunei revolt, December 1962; the officer at left wears the regiment's green and gold 'tent hat' (see Plate F4). The QRIH took over in October 1962 as the divisional reconnaissance regiment of 17th Gurkha Inf Div; in September the following year they handed over to 4th Royal Tank Regt, whose higher formation was then designated 17th British Division. (IWM FES/62/262/72)

encountered (see under Plate H1). In order to increase the reliable quick-reaction elements available to the Djakarta government, in 1961 four picked units from the three infantry regiments based in Java had been given airborne training, including 328 & 330 Para-Raider Bns, from the Kujang Regt of the Siliwongi Division.

B1: Private, A Company, 1st Battalion Queen's Own Highlanders; Seria airfield, Brunei, December 1962

Men of A Coy deplaned from two Twin Pioneer aircraft to seize Seria airfield after just one hour's training in rapid disembarkation at Labuan. This private wears a Mk III helmet with scrim camouflage; for jungle patrols the Jocks would wear jungle hats with a blue rectangular patch bearing the white St Andrew's cross at front and back. His 'olive green' (OG) shirt displays shoulder strap slides with embroidered black titles 'QO/ HIGHLANDERS', and on both sleeves the formation sign of 99 Gurkha Inf Bde – white crossed kukris on a brown rectangle. Issue OG trousers, with a map pocket on the outside of the left thigh, are confined in blancoed 37 Pattern anklets, over polished ammunition boots. His newly introduced 58 Ptn CEFO (Combat Equipment Fighting Order) comprises belt, yoke (suspenders), two 'Bren' pouches and a water bottle carrier; a World War II vintage 17in Collins machete in a light brown leather scabbard is slung behind his hip. His weapon is the 7.62mm semi-automatic L1A1 SLR (self loading rifle) which had just become standard in the British Army; weighing 9½lb, it had a detachable

43

20-round magazine. British infantry rifle training required (and still does) accurate shooting at 300 yards. (With thanks to LtCol Charles McHardy for his assistance.)

B2: Marine, 42 Commando, Royal Marines; Brunei, winter 1962/63

Nos.40 and 42 Commandos served throughout the Confrontation. L Company, 42 Cdo RM recovered the hostages at Limbang; the company was commanded by Capt John Jeremy Moore, who had already won his first MC in the Malayan Emergency, and who would become more widely known in 1982 as commander of British land forces in the Falklands campaign.

This Marine on a local patrol has folded his green Commando beret forward into a cap shape to shield his eyes. He wears the OG shirt and 'trousers drill green' with a pair of the newly issued calf-length green canvas jungle boots, with charcoal-coloured rubber soles and reinforcement. With light 58 Ptn patrol order he wears an old 37 Ptn mapcase, the flap lifted to show the acetate window covering the map folded to the area of an operation. The 9mm L2A3 Sterling sub-machine gun was a practical weapon for close range contacts in wooded terrain, weighing under 6lb empty and having a 550rpm rate of fire.

B3: Rifleman, 1st Battalion Green Jackets; Miri, North Borneo, winter 1962/63

This was the correct designation at this date, when – since 1958 – the former Oxfordshire & Buckinghamshire Light Infantry (43rd & 52nd) formed the senior battalion of the Green Jackets Brigade, alongside the former King's Royal Rifle Corps (60th) and the Rifle Brigade (95th). On 1 January 1966 these units would be amalgamated to form a 'large regiment' as 1st, 2nd & 3rd Bns The Royal Green Jackets. In 1962/63 1st Bn was commanded by LtCol 'Todd' Sweeney, who had led a platoon on D-Day when D Coy, 2nd Bn Ox & Bucks LI seized the River Orne bridges on the left flank of the Normandy beachhead.

This rifleman, about to board a helicopter for an operation, wears standard OG shirt and trousers with jungle boots, and his brigade's rifle-green beret with silver badge. He has the full field kit for an extended operation: 58 Ptn webbing, with a groundsheet in a poncho roll and a skein of heavy cord attached beneath the 'kydney pouches', a machete on his hip, and over all a 44 Ptn haversack with a 'pick, lightweight' in the shovel retaining straps. This pack was shorter and easier to wear with the crowded 58 Ptn rear belt order than the field pack of that set, which was almost invariably left on unit transport or in barracks.

C1: NCO, 3rd Battalion Royal Australian Regiment; Sarawak, June 1965

The uniform of the Australian infantryman was the 'jungle greens' introduced for all arms in 1958; the jungle hat was of the British pattern. If they were ever displayed on lanyards, 3 RAR's identifying colour was rifle-green, and 4 RAR's scarlet. Characteristically Australian items are the high, two-buckle leggings of blackened webbing; the 'boots AB' of World War II vintage, though now blackened; and the long net veil of oval-weave mesh. The webbing is basically British 37 Ptn, modified for jungle use late in World War II, although some 44 Ptn items were also made available. The 37 Ptn shoulder braces were widened to spread weight. The basic pouches are worn, with British 44 Ptn water bottles, popular for the integral aluminium mug, which could be heated for a quick 'brew' rather than bothering with messtins. The Australian machete, introduced in 1944, resembled the US type. The 'large pack' is that used by the British Army since 1908. The 9mm Owen SMG, modified in the 1950s with an added sliding plate over the rear of the receiver, was by now more often blackened than camouflage-painted; the box magazine held 33 rounds, and rate of fire was a rapid 700rpm. He is taking from its M7 'bandoleer' a US M18A1 Claymore command-detonated directional anti-personnel mine; this projected 900 ball bearings over an arc of 60°, with lethal effect out to 250 yards.

C2: Guardsman, 1st Battalion Scots Guards; boat patrol, Sabah, 1964

This figure is a composite of two members of such a patrol. He wears a bulky, awkward kapok life jacket, and 44 Ptn belt order, over his OG shirt and trousers. He has cut down the brim of his jungle hat; and, unusually, he wears 37 Ptn anklets over his jungle boots, presumably to prevent undergrowth snagging the laces – they would not be effective protection against leeches. His weapon is the US M79 40mm grenade launcher, called the 'elephant gun' by British troops. This fired HE, smoke and illumination rounds; against area targets HE was effective to 350 yards and for point targets to 150 yards.

C3: Radio operator, 1st Battalion Royal Ulster Rifles; Sarawak, July 1964

This radioman operating the standard A41 VHF platoon set may be on his first jungle operation; he has made the mistake of stripping off his shirt. The 'floppy' jungle hat bears his battalion's black band with a green shamrock sign at the front; such signs – usually simple bands or shapes in solid light colours – were used by many units for instant recognition during fleeting jungle contacts. His trousers, jungle boots and partial 44 Ptn belt order would be conventional, but as a radio operator he carries a Sterling SMG instead of a rifle. The A41 set, weighing 48lb with its spare battery and full ancillaries, is carried on the multi-purpose aluminium tubular 'general service carrier', lighter than that designed specifically for use with the A41 in Europe. He is using a plastic Slidex signal encryption wallet with a clear front. This system used variable grids of alpha-numeric codes, written in pencil on celluloid strips, to encrypt important messages such as map references, orders and intelligence reports.

D1: Trooper, D Squadron, 22nd Special Air Service Regiment; Sarawak, 1963

When the Brunei revolt broke out in December 1962 the future role of the SAS was under debate – was it to be dedicated to NATO in Europe, or to prepare for global missions? The outbreak of the revolt saw D Sqn deployed rapidly, and during the Confrontation there was always at least one British, Australian or New Zealand SAS squadron in Borneo. This trooper is depicted at a time when they were providing a 'tripwire' and pursuing a 'hearts and minds' programme in the villages along the Indonesian border. It was to be another year before the SAS began to develop their dress and equipment by improvisation and acquisitions, and apart from the cut-down jungle hat this trooper wears almost entirely standard clothing and webbing order. One difference is the belt fashioned from an air resupply stowage strap with a roller buckle; another is the backpack habitually carried – the 1944 Bergen rucksack. The LMG is the 7.62mm L4A5, rebarrelled from the old .303in Bren, and still known by that name to most soldiers. Its 500rpm rate of fire was unimpressive, but it was lighter and shorter than the GPMG, and its 30-round magazine avoided the problem of linked ammunition fouling in dirt or vegetation. We have chosen to show one modified with a forward pistol grip – apparently from an Owen gun – by a unit armourer (although the source photo in fact shows this carried by a Gurkha – see page 2).

D2: Dog handler, 2nd Battalion Green Jackets; Sarawak, 1965

This regiment's jungle hat recognition sign, when used, was a white Maltese Cross shape; these twisted lengths of white and green paracord are simply a way of 'personalizing' the hat (paracord was also used for boot laces). Three types of dogs were used in Borneo: infantry patrol dogs (as here), to alert patrols to the presence of the enemy; trackers; and war dogs, to protect installations. The handler wears standard patrol uniform and equipment; photos of 2 GJ show entire sets of 44 Ptn webbing, with the 'gollock'-shaped machete. Apart from his own kit the handler's haversack contains two 1lb tins of food for the dog and a simple veterinary kit. The officially recommended stowage for the haversack was as follows: (left outside pocket) face veil, insect repellent, foot powder, matches, water sterilizing kit, rifle cleaning box, string or paracord, and Paludrine anti-malarial tablets; (right outside pocket) small messtin half, spoon or fork, hexamine cooker, snack – tea, sugar, milk; (main compartment) 48 hours' rice etc rations, spare socks, large waterproof bag, and for section commanders a medical pack; (attached below) poncho, and for section commanders a 120ft line. A pair of gym shoes was often attached outside the pack.

D3: Punan tracker; Sarawak border, 1963

The trackers and scouts employed by the British in Borneo and mainland Malaysia were of several distinct tribal groups, and varied widely in appearance. Some – like this warrior of the Punan tribe, from the Fifth Division in eastern Sarawak – wore mostly native clothing, often simply a loincloth. He has been given a pair of khaki drill shorts; a single-barrel 12-bore Remington-action shotgun to replace his 8ft blowpipe (although with the latter he could probably hit a coin at 30 feet); and an old rifle charger bandolier to carry its cartridges. Unlike e.g. the Iban, Sea Dyak and Kayan, the Punan do not seem to practice extensive tattooing, but do stretch their earlobes, and wear multiple bangles on their arms and legs. The elaborately woven black and white fibre hat, trimmed with hornbill feathers, is typical of this tribe; they trade decorated mats with other tribes for items they cannot fashion themselves, such as this Sea Dyak *mandau* headhunter's sword secured by a woven belt. During the Confrontation some local scouts are alleged to have taken heads, as they had done during the Malayan Emergency, although officially this practice had long ceased.

E1: Lance-Naik Rambahadur Limbu (VC), C Coy, 2nd Battalion, 10th Gurkha Rifles; Gunong Tepoi, Kalimantan, 21 November 1965

The four two-battalion Gurkha regiments – 2nd, 6th, 7th and 10th Gurkha Rifles – provided about half of the infantry throughout the Confrontation. The story of the Claret

Capt Robin Adshead, Army Air Corps, with 'Celer', his Sioux AH 1 helicopter, of the AAC platoon attached to 2nd Gurkha Rifles (see Plate G2). He wears the officer's embroidered badge on a black patch on the pale blue AAC beret, a KD shirt with rank slides on the shoulder straps, OG trousers and white kid flying gloves, and carries a white Mk.3 flying helmet with a black fabric cover over the visor. In later years Robin himself would become a leading military photographer. (IWM)

operation during which L/Cpl Limbu earned his Victoria Cross is told in detail on pages 38–41. He wears standard issue jungle uniform, with his battalion's white 'X' recognition sign on the front and back of his hat. (Other Gurkha signs used apart from those on this plate included a red square by 2/2nd GR, and a yellow 'doughnut' by one battalion of 6th GR.) He wears 44 Ptn fighting order, and carries the LMG that he picked up and used instead of his US Armalite AR15 after carrying in the two mortally wounded soldiers of his gun section, Kharbakahadur Limbu and Bijuliparsad Rai.

E2: Rifleman, 1st Battalion, 10th Gurkha Rifles; Labis, Malaya, September 1964

This illustrates the 44 Ptn fighting order without the haversack. This set, made of lighter webbing than the 58 Ptn, had been specifically designed for tropical warfare and was still much in demand although officially withdrawn from service. The white 'doughnut' front and rear was 1/10th GR's recognition sign. The belt order includes two water bottles; and the 16in *kukri* knife from which the Gurkha soldier was inseparable, and which was used both for clearing brush and – when opportunity offered – in close quarter combat. Some photos show machetes also being carried. The standard weapon at this date was the SLR, but the 5.56mm AR15 (type-classified by the US Army as the M16) was coming into use and would soon be general issue.

E3: Lieutenant, 2nd Battalion, 7nd Gurkha Rifles; Lumbis, Kalimantan, June 1965

This subaltern is reconstructed as he might have appeared during the Claret operation in late June, which B Coy carried out with Australians from 1 Sqn, SASR. Clothing is conventional, and his hat bears the white recognition band of 2/7th GR. On cross-border operations unit titles and rank badges were not worn; at other times doubled shoulder straps were attached to the shirt bearing e.g. two rank pips and '7 G.R.' embroidered in black. Officers wore 44 Ptn webbing like their men, and carried rifles – either the SLR or, by 1965, the AR15; pistols were considered useless, and SMGs sometimes unreliable. Officially, a sub-unit leader and his second-in-command were supposed to carry binoculars, compass, maps and protractors; in practice binoculars were of limited value, easy to break or lose, and awkward to carry. Most British officers of Gurkha units carried the *kukri* knife. Apart from ammunition and grenades the ammo pouches also accomodated a few comforts such as chocolate bars (carried away from the body, or they melted); sometimes a pair of secateurs were carried secured by a lanyard, to cut silently through foliage during the approach to the target. The 44 Ptn haversack contained spare clothing, rations, a hammock of parachute material, the lightweight Australian groundsheet, and sometimes an Australian inflatable mattress – this was not for comfort, but for use as a stretcher for casualties. Items such as washing kit, mosquito repellent, notebooks and pens, etc, were carried in plastic bags against the damp. (With thanks for assistance to Brig, former Capt, David Morgan, 7th GR.)

F1: Warrant Officer 2nd Class, Royal Army Pay Corps

This plate illustrates examples of clean, badged OG clothing worn in rear areas and as barracks dress. With the midnight-blue general service beret bearing the 'Stabrite' badge of the RAPC, this WO2 wears laundered and starched OG shirt and shorts. Bright 'RAPC' titles are pinned to the shoulder straps, and (although it is hidden at this angle) he wears the corps' twisted primrose-yellow and blue lanyard at the left shoulder. On each upper sleeve he displays the formation sign of 17th Gurkha Inf Div – white crossed kukris on dark green. (The signs of the constituent brigades were the same apart from the background colours – red, black and brown for 48, 63 and 99 Bdes respectively.) His warrant badge is worn on a right wrist strap. A 44 Ptn belt, long khaki socks and polished black shoes complete the uniform.

F2: Sergeant, Royal Army Medical Corps

The tightly cut other ranks' 1950 pattern four-pocket bush jacket in OG Aertex was smart enough for wear in rear areas, but was uncomfortable and unpopular as a field dress. Its integral cloth waist belt was usually removed. This RAMC sergeant, contributing to the 'hearts and minds' programme, displays the cap badge and cherry-red right shoulder lanyard of his corps; bright 'RAMC' shoulder titles; and the sleeve patch of HQ Far East Land Forces above his plain white tape badges of rank. Insignia were attached with press studs or hooks-&-eyes, as the clothing required frequent laundering.

F3: Vice-Admiral Sir Peter Twiss, Royal Navy

When on shore in operational areas RN officers wore Army-issue tropical dress. In this case the Commander Far East Fleet, photographed visiting 845 NAS at Nangga Gaat, wears the officer's equivalent to the OR's bush jacket, the four-pocket 'jacket, cellular'. His full dress gold lace shoulder boards of rank have been looped to its shoulder straps, and he wears a midnight-blue beret with the RN officer's embroidered bullion cap badge – though in a slovenly manner, by Army and RM standards.

F4: Captain, Queen's Royal Irish Hussars

This captain wears the QRIH officer's traditional gold-laced green 'tent hat'. Officers used issue clothing in the field but for barracks wear they normally had uniforms privately tailored. Small variations were common, by regimental custom or private whim; this cavalry officer's 'jacket, cellular' has shaped breast pocket flaps and leather 'football' buttons. Bronze metal ranking is worn on the shoulder straps, but not regimental titles; on both sleeves he displays the 17th Gurkha Inf Div patch, and on his breast the British and UN medal ribbons for Korean War service.

G1: Petty Officer, Royal Navy landing party, 1964

This sailor was photographed leaving a Wessex helicopter on the carrier HMS *Victorious* in January 1964. He wears the naval gunnery helmet of Royal Armoured Corps pattern, painted dark grey; the light blue shirt and dark blue denim trousers of No.8 dress, and naval boots (without separate toecaps or hobnailed soles). His sleeves bear dark blue badges on white 'tombstone' patches: on his left, his PO rank – crowned crossed anchors; and on his right, the crossed cannon, between two six-point stars, all above 'A', of anti-aircraft rating 1st class. His web equipment is the RN 1919 Ptn, with added World War II-vintage pouches for the 50-round magazines of the 9mm Lanchester Mk I* SMG – venerable but visually impressive, and with a usefully robust butt for close-quarter persuasion. This was used almost exclusively by the RN, being carried by POs while sailors used

Iban tribesmen of the 'Junglewood Fighters', the Border Scout unit formed on 1 August 1963 to protect 845 NAS's helicopter base at Nangga Gat. They wear OG shirts and shorts with jungle hats, apart from the corporal at centre, who has a midnight-blue beret; the bright, pierced badge shows two native weapons crossed on a circular wreath, with a central shield. He also displays white tape rank badges and the Border Scouts shoulder title (see Plate H2). All three carry 12-bore shotguns. (IWM HU 72774)

.303in rifles and officers Webley revolvers. Unseen here, a 37 Ptn 'small pack' behind his shoulders completes the rig.

This dress and equipment is more complete than was usual for the numerous small parties deployed by coastal minehunters and river craft to search local boats. Coastal crews took full advantage of their distance from senior officers to indulge in freedom of dress; locally-made lightweight shirts and shorts in the same colours as issue No.8s were common, with canvas-and-rubber gym shoes, and any headgear from white naval caps to coolie hats (HMS *Wilkieston's* crew even indulged a craze for cowboy hats.) Army OG jungle hats, uniforms and boots were sometimes acquired. Boarding parties from coastal craft might consist of an officer (usually the first lieutenant), a PO (the coxswain) or leading seaman, a radio operator and three other ratings; they normally wore no headgear (though helmets when boarding a large vessel), shirt, shorts and gym shoes, with webbing and small arms (and minesweeper sailors were inseparable from a rigging knife and marlin spike in a leather belt holster). Cover might be offered by Bren guns mounted on the bridge. (With thanks to David Morris and Peter Down.)

G2: Sergeant helicopter pilot, 656 Sqn, Army Air Corps

The AAC flew the Scout and Sioux for light missions such as airborne command posts, and casualty and prisoner evacuation. This sergeant's rank and qualification are identified by three small white tape chevrons on the upper right sleeve, and the Army pilot's wings on the left breast (only the Army and Royal Marines train NCOs as helicopter pilots). His one-piece light drab Lightweight Flying Overalls have pairs of zipped pockets on the chest, thighs and lower legs, from one of which protrudes his folded AAC light blue beret. His outfit is completed by a Flying Helmet Mk 3, white kid flying gloves, jungle boots, and a 44 Ptn belt with a holstered 9mm Browning pistol hooked to its ammunition pouch.

G3: Lance-Corporal, 15 Air Despatch Regiment, Royal Army Service Corps; Kuching, 1964

This despatcher on the airfield wears the RASC badge on his midnight-blue beret; a one-piece cotton denim overall in a drab olive shade, with pockets at left breast and thigh only; and a pair of the popular 'hockey boots'. Round his neck are a parachute-nylon scarf, and a lanyard securing a 9mm pistol holstered on a 44 Ptn belt (as on Plate G2) – this would usually be discarded when in flight, so as not to snag on pallet straps. The brassard on his left shoulder displays his AD qualification wings, the patch of 15 AD Regt (a gold-yellow Dakota on royal blue), and his badge of rank. The regimental patch was also worn on the right shoulder, or alternatively on the left breast only. (With thanks to Vic Wright.)

H1: Company Sergeant Major, B Company, 2nd Bn The Parachute Regiment; Plaman Mapu, 27 April 1965

The action for which CSM Williams was awarded the DCM is described on pages 21–22 (this reconstruction does not pretend to be a portrait of his features); his wounds cost him his left eye and the hearing in his left ear. Williams was roused from sleep by the first attack, and ran out wearing only OG trousers and hastily-grabbed jungle boots and 58 Ptn webbing; initially he used his SLR, but later fired a GPMG from the hip, with a long belt of 7.62mm link (the 'Jimpy' weighs 24lb and has an 800rpm rate of fire.)

Royal Marine commandos, tired but satisfied after returning from a cross-border 'Claret' operation. Their light belt order is constructed from cargo pallet straps with roll-pin quick release buckles. Two have face veils as sweat rags, and all retain traces of camouflage cream. On patrol men went unwashed and unshaven, since the smell of Western soap was distinctive in the jungle and might give a patrol away to an alert enemy. The 5.56mm AR15 rifle was generally used in the jungle by this date; its alloy and plastic components made it 30 per cent lighter than the SLR, and though the bullet was almost two-thirds lighter it had about 100m/s greater muzzle velocity. (RM Museum)

The attackers were two companies of the 3rd Bn of the Indonesian Army's *Regimen Para-Komando Angatan Darat* (RPKAD) based in Solo, central Java. The RPKAD was an elite force; it had seen action, including several combat jumps, during an anti-government rising in Sumatra in 1958, and in Dutch-held West Irian (Irian Jaya) in 1962. During the Confrontation elements of its three battalions trained local dissidents as well as mounting cross-border operations. Later prominent in the anti-communist civil war of 1965–67, the regiment was expanded and redesignated, initially as KOPASSANDHA (1971) and later as KOPASSUS (1985).

H2: Iban Border Scout attached to 2nd Battalion, 10th Gurkha Rifles, 1965

Scouts might go naked apart from loincloths, or wear odds and ends of European clothing; indistinguishable from the local villagers, they were a valuable source of intelligence on Indonesian border movements. As time passed and their status was formalized some were issued uniforms, 44 Ptn webbing and weapons. Note the shoulder title worn here, 'BORDER SCOUTS' in yellow on a long green arc with a double yellow edging; a shoulder patch featuring the indigenous hornbill bird was sometimes worn in camp, as were British rank chevrons and a badged dark blue beret. Note this Iban's lavish tribal tattooing, typically extending all over the torso and limbs. His weapon is the .303in No.5 rifle – the jungle carbine version of the Lee Enfield.

The Indonesians obtained their weapons and ordnance – including mines – from many sources. At the scout's feet, made safe and laid aside for disposal, is a US M2A4 'bounding' anti-personnel mine. Lifted mines were either marked with white tape, or covered with a sprung cloth pyramid marker.

INDEX

Figures in **bold** refer to illustrations.

Adshead, Capt Robin 45
air combat 18–19, **19**
air drops 19, 20
armoured cars **15, 17, 43**
artillery **42**
Australian forces 17–18
    SAS 10
        Claret Operations 35–7

Barton, Brig F.C. 19
Beale, Lt Patrick 17
Bearing, Maj R.S. 37
Birdsong, Operation 16
Black Cobra Battalion 14
Border Scouts 9, 10, **10, 11,** 24, **46**
Borneo 3, 7, 17
    north border area **8**
British forces 5, 7, 10
    see also Australian forces; Gurkha forces; New Zealand forces
    medical aid to Indonesians 9, 10
    operational principles 7–8
    tactics 19–23
Brunei, Sultanate of 4, 7, 10, 15, 35
    revolt (1962) 4–6
Bukit Knuckle base 20
Byers, Lt 17

Calvert, Michael 9
Cameron, Maj I.D. **7**
Chamberlin, Lt Peter 20
Clandestine Communist Organization (CCO) 11, 41
Claret Operations 24, 33–8
Clements, LtCol 12
colonial powers 3
Commonwealth forces 10
communist insurgencies
    Malaya 3
Creighton, Sgt Bob 13
Cross, Maj John 10, 11

dog patrols 16
Dwikova, Operation 16

Erskine-Tulloch, Capt 34

Federal Reconnaissance Regiment 10
Fleet Air Arm (FAA) 10, 12
footwear 35
forts, jungle 19–20, **22**
    patrolling from 22–3, **33**
Fraser, Rifleman Terry **5**
Freefall, Operation 33

Green Jackets (GJ) 5, 9, 20–1, **34**
Guong Tepoi 38–41, **40**
Gurkha forces **2**, 5, 7, 8, 9, 11–12, 13, 14, 15, 16, **18,** 20, 22, 24, 33, 37, 38–41
    see also British forces

Haddow, Maj R. 16
Harrison, Tom 9
Healey, Dennis 24, 42
'hearts and minds operations' 8–10
helicopters **2**, 10, 12, 14, 16, **17,** 18, 19, 38, **39, 45**
Horner, David 35

Indonesia-based Border Terrorists (IBTs) 8, **11, 12, 13**

attacks by (1963-64) 11–15
Indonesian Communist Party (PKI) 41
Indonesian forces **4,** 7, 11
    Air Force paratroops (PGT) 15–16, **18**
    attacks by (1964-65) 15–19, 20–2
    ground troops 15–16

Jackson, Gen Sir William 4, 6, 18
Jackson, Pte 17
'JAK' (*London Evening Standard* cartoonist) 18–19
James Bond, Operation 33–4

Kalabakan attack 12–13
Kedayan tribe 4
Keen Edge, Operation 10
Kellway-Bamber, LtCol 10

Lea, MajGen George 10, 42
Limbu, LCpl Rambahadur **E1**(29), 38–41, **41,** 45
Long Jawai attack 11–12
Long Miau attack 13–14

McHardy, LtCol W.G. **7**
Malaya 3
Malayan, North Borneo and Sarawak Police Field Forces 8, 11
Malaysia, Federation of 3, 7
    attacks on
        (1963–64) 11–15
        (1964–65) 15–19, 38
Maphilindo 3, 4
Marshall, Lt Tom 36
Mayman, Maj 14
Meldrum, Maj W.J.D. 37
Miers, Lt Christopher 20
Moloney, Maj D.W.S. 38
Moore, Capt Jeremy 5
mortars 23

Nantakor garrison 24
Nasution, Gen 41
Naval Air Squadron (NAS) 12, 18, 39
naval forces 10, **14**
New Guinea 17
New Zealand forces 16, 17
    SAS
        Claret Operations 37–8
Newell, Dare 9
North Kalimantan National Army (Tentara Nasional Kalimantan Utara) (TNKU) 4–6, 7, 8, 11

Parachute Regiment 21–2, 36
Pasley-Tyler, Lt Robert 9
Patawari, Maj Audy 14
Peele, Lt Michael 13
Plaman Mapu base 21–2

Queens Own Highlanders 5
Queen's Royal Irish Hussars 14, **43**

Rahman, Tunku Abdul 3–4, 6
Razak, Tun 13
river patrols 37
Roderick, Lt Trevor 10
Royal Australian Regiment (RAR) 17
Royal Malay Regiment (RMR) 10
Royal Marine Commandos 5, 12, 24, 33, 34, **36, 47**
Royal New Zealand Regiment (RNZR) 16, 17

Sabah 7, 33
Sabre Tooth, Operation 14

Sarawak 7, 15, 17, 19, 23, 34, 35
SAS (Special Air Service) 8–10, 13, 24
    Claret Operations 34–5
    tactics 23
SAS Phantoms of the Jungle (Horner) 35–6
SBS (Special Boat Squadron) 12, 24, 33
Scots Guards 37
Search and Rescue Beacons (SARBE) 36
Sebatik Island 33
Seeger, Lt R.A.M. 33
Sherman, LtCdr G.J. 18
Singapore 3, 7, 15
Smith, Brig E.D. 'Birdie' 24
South-East Asia **4**
Stass base 20–1
Subandrio, Dr 4, 13
Suharto, Gen 41
Sukarno, President Achmad 3, 4, 6, 14, 41
Sweeney, Col H.J. 6

Tawau Assault Group (TAG) 12, 24
Templer, FM Sir Gerald 9
Tentara Nasional Kalimantan Utara (North Kalimantan National Army) (TNKU) 4–6, 7, 8, 11
Thakeray, Sgt 19
TNKU (Tentara Nasional Kalimantan Utara) North Kalimantan National Army 4–6, 7, 8, 11
Track attack 14
Twiss, VAdm Sir Peter **F3**(30), 46

uniforms
    Border Scout **H2**(32), 47
    Capt, Queen's Royal Irish Hussars **F4**(30), 46
    CSM, Parachute Regiment **H1**(32), 47
    Dog handler, Green Jackets **D2**(28), 45
    Guardsman, Scots Guards **C2**(27), 44
    LCpl, Royal Army Service Corps **G3**(31), 47
    LCpl Limbu, Gurkha Rifles **E1**(29), **41,** 45
    Lt, Gurkha Rifles **E3**(29), 46
    NCO, Indonesian Army paratrooper **A3**(25), 43
    NCO, Royal Australian Regiment **C1**(27), 44
    PO, RN **G1**(31), 46–7
    Pte, Queen's Own Highlanders **B1**(26), 43–4
    Radio Operator, Royal Ulster Rifles **C3**(27), 44
    Rifleman, Green Jackets **B3**(26), 44
    Rifleman, Gurkha Rifles **E2**(29), 45
    Royal Marine Commando **B2**(26), 44
    Sgt, Helicopter Pilot **G2**(31), 47
    Sgt, Indonesian Air Force **A2**(25), 43
    Sgt, Royal Army Medical Corps **F2**(30), 46
    TNKU officer **A1**(25), 43
    Tracker, Punan tribe **D3**(28), 45
    Trooper, SAS **D1**(28), 44–5
    VAdm Sir Peter Twiss, RN **F3**(30), 46
    Warrant Officer, Royal Army Pay Corps **F1**(30), 46
United Nations 3, 7, 13

Victoria Cross award 38–41
Vietnam 3, 42

Walker, MajGen Walter **7,** 7–8, 10, 15, 19, 23, 24, 42
Willoughby, Maj Digby 24
Wilson, Harold 24, 42
Wogimen, SgtMaj 16
Woodhouse, LtCol John 8–9, 23

Yassin Affendi 4, 8